The V
Tina

Cover design by Jennifer Ricker,
Left Ear Design
www.lefteardesign.com

Published by OCRS, Inc.

Library of Congress
Control Number: 2005931584

ISBN 0-9725796-8-0

Printed in the United States of America

To obtain more copies of this book, go to
www.somestillserve.com
or write
OCRS, Inc.
P.O. Box 551627
Jacksonville, FL 32255

i

Featured Author, The Library Guild
2005 Much Ado About Books

*"...Cribbs' eloquent command of time and place
puts the reader squarely into his mind's eye..."*
Halifax Magazine

*"...Randy Cribbs is vibrantly alive inside
each of his books..."*
Flager Magazine

"...Cribbs is becoming quite a prolific writer..."
St. Augustine Record

*"Randy Cribbs' fifth book speaks to mystery
lovers on many levels. It is an exploration of one of history's
foggy corners combined with a punchy, satisfying whodunit, set in
modern day St. Augustine. I've never read anything quite so original and would recommend it as a good read."*
Peter Guinta, Senior Writer,
St. Augustine Record

*". . . his passion for the area's history, architecture and colorful
characters-past and present-provide endless inspiration. . .such a
craftsman and really works hard at getting it clean and clear for
the reader. . . with Randy, it is all about vision..."*
The St. Johns Sun

*"Randy Cribbs has stretched his expansive imagination in this tale
of modern day events combined with a touch of early Florida history...St. Augustine is the perfect setting for this intriguing story,
and readers will recognize the places and characters he so vividly
describes. In the end readers will be posed with the question: was
Ponce DeLeon pursuing the wrong object for everlasting youth?*

*Jim Mast, Author of
'Bloody Sunset in St. Augustine.'*

THE VESSEL

tinaja

An Ancient City Mystery

*TO: Lynne
From the old
town to you,
So good to see you,
Randy Cribb
2009*

RANDY CRIBBS

OCRS, Inc., Jacksonville, Florida

OCRS, Inc. is proud to publish
These books by Randy Cribbs:

'Were You There: Vietnam Notes'
'Tales From The Oldest City'
'One Summer In The Old Town'
'Illumination Rounds'
(co-authored with Peter Guinta)
'The Vessel'

Cover designs created by Jennifer V. Ricker,
Lefteardesign.com, winner of the 2003,
2004, and 2005
PhotoshopWorld Guru Award for Website Design.
Format and technical design by Matt Cribbs, Left Ear Design

Vessel- 1. utensil for holding something as a vase, bowl, pot, kettle, etc. 2. a person thought of as being the receiver or repository of some spirit or influence.

Webster's New World College
Dictionary, Fourth Edition

Dedicated to Edna,
with love.
Thanks Mom.

Prologue

May 9, 2002

    Robert corrected a misspelled word and reached for a cigarette, then remembered he didn't smoke anymore.

    It was a good story, and it had all the elements: mystery, supernatural happenings, murder, romance. The stuff of any good work of fiction. The story spanned centuries from Old Florida to present—Indians included! He felt good about it! Then he remembered his promise to the priest, and his friend.

    Could he convince the old man that it was highly improbable anyone would piece the events and characters together and recognize that what happened a few weeks ago in the nation's oldest city was even remotely connected to his story.

    And what about the detective? What if he read the story? Could he put the pieces together?

    He inserted a disc and hit save. The 'save as' icon appeared.

    Maybe he should call the priest now; appeal to his friend's logic. But, he had been so adamant! And what about all the others? What would they say?

    Even if someone did recognize one of the characters

as real, the story was too incredible for anyone to possibly believe. Supernatural power! Immortality! Unexplainable events! Strange deaths! This is the twenty-first century. No one would buy it!

Looking from the outside in, there was just no way a sane person would believe it.

But, as the priest had warned, what if someone did—searched for it—and found it?

What if it did show up again and someone put the pieces together? It happened before. Could it happen again?

The vessel had impacted many lives over the centuries—even his own. Men he had known, and many others, were dead because of their greed.

What should he do? No writer in his right mind would allow a good story to go untold, and this was a great story! Telling it would not resurrect the vessel.

Robert leaned back and stared at the ceiling, counting the holes in one of the tiles as the events of the last few weeks played out again in his mind. They were in the computer, and although he could erase them with the stroke of a finger, they would still be in his head.

The cursor blinked, awaiting his command.

CHAPTER 1

Circa 1500

The animal sounds of a primitive land echoed through the early morning stillness. Some almost hushed, as if not wanting to call attention to their presence. A spring mist hung gently in the air, quieting the footsteps of foragers and partially camouflaging their scent from other creatures – those who preferred meat over berries.

Florida was an unconquered wilderness; a land that presented a daily struggle for its creatures and the few Indian tribes who shared the rivers and swamps with them. It was a balanced relationship with man and beast living in a harmony of survival, each becoming the aggressor only when food was needed or territory threatened. The young white tailed deer moving through a dense thicket was a forager, occupied with tender green shoots as the July sun crept slowly upward.

The buck moved cautiously forward, stopping frequently to lift his majestic head, sniffing the air for unfriendly scents. He stepped from the thicket into a sparsely wooded area where the grass was fuller, greener from more exposure to the sun.

The low, crunching sound of roots being pulled from the ground by the young buck was interrupted by a slight clunk as his hoof struck an object on the ground. He paused and sniffed the object curiously. Deciding it was not edible, he turned his attention back to the more familiar vegetation, but his keen senses had been diverted just long enough. Suddenly, his head lifted, nose flared, instinctively knowing something was wrong, but it was too late.

Two hundred feet away, the young Timucua stood like a statue, the muscles in his dark arms taunt from the pressure of his bow at full draw. As the buck raised his head, the arrow made a swishing sound, audible in the quiet woods as it headed for the target. Simultaneously, the warrior ran toward the buck, unsheathing the crude knife at his side as he ran.

The buck, arrow imbedded in his throat, fell to his front knees. As he attempted to rise, the Indian was on his back, thrusting the knife deep into the deer's heart. With a low bellow, the buck fell, his life ebbing away. Nijo caressed the buck's thick fur, almost lovingly, in tribute to his fallen brother.

Nijo rose, shattering the quiet with a yell as he held his hands high, bloody from the killing thrust. He moved to position the deer for dressing but stopped when his bare foot stepped on the object that had been the buck's downfall. Squatting, he laid the knife to one side and picked up the strange looking object. He studied the unique shape of his find, noting the flat bottom and smooth surface. He set the object down and peered into its hollow interior, about five inches deep. The rim was rounded, smooth to his touch. Unsure of what to make of this thing, he picked it up, retrieved his knife and struck the surface with the blade; not bone or wood, he decided. Grunting, he set it down again and reached to cut the deer's throat, his free hand cupped to catch the first blood for the ritual drinking that was a part of the kill. As he slashed, the blood poured into his hand and the partially upright vessel on the ground. He quickly adjusted the vessel to catch the blood. When it was half full, he stood and studied the red liquid, and then with another yell, he lifted it to his lips and drank deeply, blood trickling down his cheeks and neck. A tingling sensation coursed through his body. He lowered the vessel, a smile playing about his handsome face as he again studied his strange find. His smile turned into a big grin as he decided what to do. He would give it to his father, the Utina tribe chief. Drinking vessels, called tinaja, were very personal to the Timucua. Shells were usually used, the whelk preferred, and when the person died, all his possessions were burned except the tinaja. Satisfied, he placed the strange vessel into the leather pouch hanging from his waist and set about dressing his kill.

The sun was beginning to set as Nijo neared his village. His strong shoulders ached from his load of fresh deer meat. The pungent odor of roasting cocina leaves used for the tea consumed daily smelled good. He could hear the whomp, whomp, whomp from the mortar-like hollowed out logs used to convert maize kernels into flour. A yell came from the village when a young boy spotted him. Several other villagers ran toward the boy, some grabbing bows or hatchets, a precaution necessary until a friend or foe status was determined.

Following the boy's pointing finger, several other villagers started yelling as they recognized Nijo and saw the fresh meat strapped to his back. Women clothed only in deerskin wrapped loosely around their waist and knotted over their left thigh began scurrying around fires, preparing spits for the feast to come. All would share the kill, as was the custom and necessity of the tribe.

As Nijo approached the center of the camp, relieved of his burden by other men, an old man made his way out of the small, crawl size opening of the largest of several crude huts. It was Parucusi, Nijo's father and chief of the tribe.

Parucusi gazed through watery eyes at the commotion. His failing eyes finally recognized Nijo, his favorite of many children. He grimaced as he straightened his stiff, aching back. I'm too old, he thought, reaching out with his wrinkled, leathery arm for the feather adorned spear leaning against the hut. The spear, once his weapon of choice in many battles, now served more as a crutch to assist his slow movement.

As Nijo approached, Parucusi watched his graceful strides with pride and some envy. The young warrior's lean, hard body reminded the chief of better times, when his reputation as a great warrior was known throughout the primitive land. Now, he was just an old man, content with peace, discouraging the young men of the tribe from confrontations with neighboring tribes.

He placed a hand on Nijo's shoulder as his son stopped.

"You did well, my son."

"Yes, father, our brother will fill many bellies this night."

"And what of the Oconi and Potano?" the old man asked, referring to the neighboring tribes.

"My kill was dressed before those old women left their huts." The young man answered with a smile.

"Come, sit with me," Parucusi said as he gently eased his tired body to the ground. "I worry when you hunt alone," he added.

"I am the son of the great Utina chief. The forest pro-

6

tects me. Our enemies fear me."

"Maybe, but not all are content with peace. You must be careful." He reached for the large shell lying by a water container made of hollowed wood. As he raised the half full shell to his mouth, Nijo spoke, "Wait, father. I have a gift for you." He reached into his pouch and removed the prize.

Taking the shell from his father's hand, he offered the vessel.

The old man took the gift, turning it as he examined the unusual shape. He scratched at the surface with a fingernail then tapped it gingerly with his knuckle.

"What is it?" He finally asked.

Proudly, Nijo turned the old man's hand upright and poured water from the shell into its hollowed out interior.

"Drink, Father."

Parucusi moved the vessel back and forth, up and down, then swirled the water around, looking for some sign that would reveal the nature of the object.

Finally, he raised the container to his lips and sipped tentatively. He smacked his lips and drank deeper. Looking at his proud son, he smiled and drank again, deeper still.

"Where did my son get this strange vessel?" He finally spoke.

"It was a gift from our brother, the deer."

"It is not wood, or stone, or horn of our brothers." He examined the vessel again. "It is not of our land."

"No. It will be easier for my father to drink from, and its surface gives pleasure when touched." He paused, then added, "Do you feel it, father?"

The old chief now fondled the vessel in both hands, caressing its smooth rim and warm surface. "Yes, I do." He nodded his head toward the young man. "I am pleased with your gift. It will be my tinaja."

"Good," Nijo responded, "now, I must see my woman, and then we will feast together."

Parucusi smiled knowingly. "Yes, it will be a good night. I will dance."

Surprised, Nijo sat back and surveyed his father. "Dance," he exclaimed, "you have not danced for many seasons."

"I will dance tonight," the chief replied, holding the vessel high. His son's gift made him feel good. It seemed to grow warmer in his hand each time he sipped the liquid, and he could feel his old body tingle. He felt somehow different.

Suddenly, he rose to his feet, the vessel still in his hand. "I will walk to the stream before the feast," he announced, starting off.

"Father, your spear," Nijo reminded the old man, knowing he was prone to stumble and could not see well.

The old man stopped, surprised. He looked around, through clear eyes, noting the bright orange sunset, cooking fires blazing, children running, excited about the coming feast. He felt good. Looking back toward his son, he smiled. "Tonight, I will walk without my friend, the spear."

Nijo watched his father walk off with quick strides.

"Nijo." His confusion was interrupted by his wife, calling from the doorway of their hut, an inviting smile highlighting her beautiful face.

Glancing again at his father, already moving out of the village to the stream, he shook his head and turned his attention to the striking woman who waited for him.

Dawn broke on a quiet camp. The feast, always a social occasion enjoyed by the entire village, had lasted late.

Nijo awoke to early morning voices, their conversation almost loud in the still sleeping camp. Recognizing his father's voice, he gently moved his sleeping wife's arm from his chest and stepped outside.

His father was listening impatiently to Iniha, the chief's village administrator and toolmaker. It was he who enjoyed the role of teacher to the young for learning the material and craft of making what they needed to hunt, to live, to survive.

Iniha was animated as he spoke, pointing occasionally to the vessel Nijo's father was holding. Iniha quietened as Nijo approached, a sign of respect for the first born of their great chief, who would also be chief one day.

"This old woman cannot do a simple job anymore," Parucusi said to Nijo.

"I did not say that, Great Chief," Iniha responded defensively. "The vessel is unlike any material I have seen. It is very hard and I fear my chief will not be pleased with my work."

"You wish to change my gift, father?"

"No, my son, it is the best gift I have ever received, but I wish to put my mark on it so that all will know it belongs to the Holato." Parucusi said, using the word for head chief.

"Iniha, you have carved the feather of our brother many times on our chief's weapons. Surely you can do this on a simple vessel." Nijo reached for the vessel, but his father pulled his hand back in a protective manner.

"I told our great chief I would try, but I am unsure of this material – what will happen," Iniha broke the uneasy silence.

"That is all you can do," replied Nijo, whose fierce loyalty and love of his tribe now instinctively moved him into his role of arbitrator, problem solver, and counselor to his people, a fact that his father had always been proud of.

"I do not require a young buck to settle my differences," Parucusi spit out, surprising the other two men.

"No, my father, I was only. . ."

"You will work here, in front of my hut, old woman, where I can see your progress. The vessel will not leave this place. Go get your tools. Carve my mark here." He pressed the vessel over the feather tattoo on his arm.

Parucusi gasped. His face lifted upward, eyes dazed. His muscles twitched as he pressed the vessel harder against his skin.

"Father!" Nijo yelled, grabbing the chief's arm.

The old man's body relaxed. He pulled the vessel away from his arm.

"Father, the tinaja..." Nijo said, eyes fixed on the vessel.

Parucusi raised the tinaja. A sinister smile creased his face when he saw his feather on its surface.

Iniha scurried away as Nijo glanced at the vessel, clutched tightly by his father.

"You do not feel well this day, father." Nijo said, trying to ease the mood. "Maybe too much dancing at the feast," he added, eyes still fixed on the tinaja.

Parucusi admired his mark on the smooth surface of the vessel.

"It is a sign." He said simply, placing the vessel carefully into his leather pouch.

"I feel good. I will hunt today. He turned to his hut, then added, "Only I may drink of the vessel. Tell all."

Nijo did not answer. He had been very proud when his gift had pleased his father, but this magic...his father's behavior...

"Yes, my father," he finally answered.

The years passed and many things changed. Nijo, now graying, had sons of his own. His father still lived, and ruled, to the amazement of all. But he had changed. The once peace-loving chief exerted his power at every opportunity and the tribe's love for him had changed to grudging respect. The tribe was in a perpetual state of war with their neighbors. The Timucua way of war had changed too. The quick raids with few casualties, more a game than war, was now battles of annihilation, led by Parucusi. Young warriors had died fighting his provoked battles with their one-time peaceful neighbors. While others aged, and many births occurred, Parucusi remained the same. The tribal chief had lived longer than two men and the tribe's numbers had increased as other tribes fell under his reign after bloody battles.

Nijo somehow felt responsible for the unhappy mood of his people because he could not shake from his thoughts the coincidence of his father's change and Nijo's gift to him many years ago – the vessel now bearing the eagle feather, mark of the chief. The vessel never left his person, and each time he drank from it, his appearance and mood frightened Nijo.

Now, summoned to his father's hut, he was worried, and upon entering, his fears were confirmed.

"Gather our warriors, we will spill the blood of the Oconi," his father greeted him without ceremony.

"But Father, they have done us no harm, and the tribe grows weary of war."

"You question me, your chief?" Parucusi demanded to know.

"No, Father, I just . . ."

11

"We leave tomorrow," Parucusi cut him off. "Antipola will go with us. It is time he tasted our enemies' blood," he added, referring to Nijo's oldest son, almost a man.

Nijo could not swallow. He knew this day would come. His son would be excited for he had never known peace. He longed to be a warrior because that was the way of the tribe. Nijo felt dread as he sighed and turned to leave, knowing his arguments, like so many others these past years, would fall on deaf ears.

The pungent smell of smoke from smoldering campfires was heavy as Nijo's warriors positioned themselves around the Oconi camp, awaiting the signal to attack. Nijo glanced around at the young men, weapons at the ready, hair pulled tight on top of their heads, a challenge to others to try to take their scalp. His gaze fell on his son, eyes wide with fear and excitement. The look saddened him. He caught Parucusi's stare, waiting impatiently. Nijo looked for a sign that would change his intent, but saw only a man intent on conquering. His father touched the vessel hanging in the leather pouch around his waist. He raised his spear. Nijo rose, suddenly tired, and took aim on the lone sentry. As the Oconi sentry fell, clutching the arrow in his throat, the warriors charged the camp. The battle quickly evolved into close-in combat, knives and hatchets cutting through the morning mist. Blood from deep fingernail gashes grown long for that purpose poured from opponents foreheads into their eyes, blinding them. Nijo pulled his knife from the chest of an Oconi warrior. Turning, he saw his son standing over a fallen warrior, his hatchet held loosely by his side, guard down, as if in shock. Running to the young boy, he shook his shoulders and grabbed his arm, half dragging him along. As they rounded a hut, they saw his father locked in a struggle with

12

the Oconi chief, a young, stronger warrior. He ran toward the two men as their sweaty bodies fell to the ground, rolling over a smoldering fire. Burned, his father's grip on his opponent loosened. The stronger man plunged his knife into Parucusi's throat, killing him instantly.

The Oconi chief struggled upright, gasping for air as Nijo arrived. The two men eyed each other cautiously. Nijo's instinct told him to lunge, while the chief was weakened, and he could see in the other man's eyes that he knew he was disadvantaged. Instead, Nijo dropped his guard. His eyes never left the other man as he kneeled by his father and touched his lifeless body. He rose slowly, facing the other chief. "My father, the great chief Parucusi is dead. We will fight no more."

The two men stared at each other in silence, the noise of the battle around them subsiding, as others saw the two chiefs standing, guards down.

"Your chief has fought for many years." The chief finally spoke.

"We will fight no more," Nijo repeated.

"What of the great chief's vessel, with the feather of our brother, the eagle?" The Oconi chief asked.

His reference to the vessel was founded on Parucusi's custom over the years of drinking the blood of his enemies after a battle was won. Nijo was saddened to learn that this behavior was known to other tribes. It was an act he long despised.

Kneeling, Nijo yanked the leather pouch from his father's waist.

"The vessel has died with my father. They will be buried together."

The Oconi chief, now facing his equal, saw in Nijo's

eyes a man of honor, a new chief who looked for peace. He nodded and lifted his hand high with a yell, causing his warriors to pause. Nijo followed suit, then sheathed his knife so that all could see.

"We will take our dead and live in peace with all our brothers."

"Take your father." The Oconi chief replied, as he turned to restore his village.

Nijo turned as he felt a hand touch his shoulder. He looked into the sad eyes of his young son.

"Father, I do not like war."

"That is good, my son. We will live in peace and hunt the great deer and fish the rivers." He glanced down at his father.

"You did not know your grandfather, our chief, before the vessel. He was a good man, but I gave him evil in the vessel. Man must never drink from it again. I will guard it and one day you will guard it. Do you understand?"

"But, Father, why not throw it into the great river so no man can have it," the boy asked.

"No!" Nijo said sharply. "I found the vessel, others can find it. Nijo and the sons of Nijo will guard it. Forever. Its power will not tempt us to drink. You will remember this always. Look at these dead, and the many dead before. Remember. The Utina will guard the vessel from all men. It is possessed...hitiquiry," he said, using the Timucua word for evil spirit. "Tell me you will do this and your sons, the future chiefs of the great Utina tribe, will do this."

The young boy looked around and met his father's eyes. "Yes, Father, we will guard the vessel, always."

The new Utina chief knelt by his father. "Come, we will take our chief home."

CHAPTER 2

April, 2002

The police detective stood on the center span of the old bridge, oblivious to the cars behind him waiting patiently for the large sailboat to pass through its open jaws. He gripped the bridge rails and leaned his upper body toward the water as the curious vehicle occupants watched. Could a person fall over accidentally and if so, would the fall kill them?

He glanced east, toward the city marina where the floating body had been found. His initial inquiries revealed that currents and tide could have taken the body from this vicinity to the marina area, if indeed he had gone over the rail. Beyond that, he had very little information to pursue in this case.

The coroner had been of little help. The body had been in the water two to three days. Some bruising, but no way to tell whether the bruises and scratches were caused by objects in the water or inflicted by another person. Cause of death; drowning. Did he have a murder or an accident? Though early in the investigation, the seasoned detective knew this would not be an open and shut case. The victim profile he had begun developing had already created too many questions. Questions he knew may never be answered.

He jotted a note on his pocket size memo pad and

headed down the walkway to his car. The thought of 'unsolved' stamped on this case did not sit well with him, and he had too much experience to even consider that possibility so early. But he also knew he needed help. From where, or whom? Always the hard question.

Three blocks away, Robert Robson stared at the last page of an article he was writing, willing it to give him the final paragraph. He focused on the black ink against the white page. No help there, either.

He leaned back in his comfortable, 1940's era slat back, rocker desk chair. Though out of place in the modern '02's, and dangerous, particularly if he moved to rise quickly from the spring loaded leaning position, Robert couldn't seem to part with the beast. After trying countless others over the years, he still liked the way his six-foot frame fit the curved wood back. The chair had thrown him more than one time over the years, and Robert had secretly named it Bronco while in one of his more philosophical moods, and Robert was, like many writers, sometimes philosophical.

In his fifties, Robert's graying hair, considered by some distinguished, was highlighted by a deep tan, the product of frequent outings in the Florida sun. Divorced many years ago, he lived alone in his south St. George Street apartment, overlooking Lake Santa Maria in the downtown area of St. Augustine. The apartment was actually one of two upstairs dwellings in a large turn of the century Victorian style house. The place, view and location suited his somewhat bohemian lifestyle. Most downtown areas were within easy walking distance, a mode he enjoyed because of his affection and attachment to America's oldest city.

He had left his native St. Augustine at the request of Uncle Sam for a few years during the Vietnam conflict and again shortly after his divorce to pursue freelance writing as he traveled the world, but missed the atmosphere and intrigue of his birthplace, and soon returned.

Still freelancing, he was currently having one of those nights when he seriously questioned his sanity for the obsession he had with writing. Though he made his living writing magazine articles, newspaper features, and editing the work of others, his real passion was writing what he philosophically called 'real' things – books. Six books had been published and provided a modest supplemental income, but many others in manuscript form lay scattered on his old library table.

And, of course, he was waiting for the perfect story; another curse he shared with most writers.

Robert simply loved writing. Some months when finances were tight, the temptation to return to newspaper or magazine employment would surface, though only briefly, because to him writing stories was a search of the soul, a capturing of life and experience to share with the world. But the real reason was that he simply loved it. However, because he enjoyed eating and freelancing supported that habit, there never seemed to be enough time for his preferred writing pursuits. In some ways, he knew this caused him to appear selfish to his many friends when he would decline various entertainment offers, preferring instead to sit behind his computer. Thankfully though, he knew most of them also understood, since this was often the subject of many friendly discussions. Robert was who he was, and his philosophical, if not always logical view was either understood or it wasn't. Balancing consideration for friends and family against those items listed in his mental must do or want to do column was not easy, but where writing was concerned, the scale usually tipped toward his side.

He let out a long breath. Rising from the Bronco ever so carefully, he opened his veranda door and stepped into the gentle April breeze, letting it caress his face.

The sound of a horse carriage on the old brick street was music to his ears. It was a sound he never grew tired of, particularly late at night when, if he listened carefully, he could almost hear the clink of sabers as soldiers walked the streets.

He watched as the carriage stopped directly below him. A middle-aged tourist climbed up and lifted his lady into the old plush carriage seat, the Matanzas Bay breeze gently blowing her hair as she nestled under the man's arm. He heard the driver cluck softly to start the old horse toward the twinkling lights of the 312 bridge in the distance. The night was silent, save for the slow clippity-clop of the horse's hooves as he plodded along, destined for the turns and twists of the old city streets, past copper domes, narrow steeples and haunting old buildings that was this place Robert loved.

Robert smiled as he thought of Eve and the many times they had enjoyed such excursions. His high school sweetheart and long time friend remained very special to him. Also divorced, they still enjoyed little outings, dinner, and occasionally evenings of a more intimate nature. They each saw friends of the opposite gender, but still, theirs was a special relationship with many good memories. Robert had thought about marriage possibilities, but his lifestyle seemed to fit, and besides, he now mused, Eve seemed to still be hung up on a mutual friend, asshole, as Robert thought of him. She and the 'other guy' had had a tumultuous relationship for years and their mutual friends felt she was crazy for putting up with the heavy drinking, abusive clown but, he thought, who can explain women.

Robert's trek down memory lane and the unfair world of love and triangles was interrupted by the ringing phone. Turning, he strolled back to his desk where he noted the ringing seemed to match the cadence of the blinking cursor. Maybe an omen, he thought.

"Hello."

"Robert, Kyle."

"Kyle, what's up, ink man?" Kyle, his good friend and senior reporter for the local mullet wrapper, newspaper to some, was always a pleasure to hear from.

"Same-o, same-o, how 'bout you?" The New Jersey transplant, now a true St. Augustinian, responded.

"Trying to do a little writing. The usual."

"I hope it's the book review," his friend said.

Oh crap, he thought. He had become so involved with his latest book attempt and the stupid article currently perplexing him the last couple of days, he forgot about a book review Kyle had asked him to do.

"Oh, yeah, man, just about through," Robert said, hoping his little white lie sounded legitimate.

After a brief pause, Kyle laughed. "You asshole, you haven't even started, have you?"

Kyle tried to throw his friend as much work as possible because he admired his writing style as well as his fishing ability, a pastime they enjoyed together. But he also knew Robert's propensity to get totally wrapped up with more 'pressing' matters and let things slip.

"Don't worry, boss man, I'll have it. Don't I always deliver?"

"Yeah, I guess you do, but I need it in two days, OK?"

"No problem."

"So prepare me, is it a decent book or can I look forward to another Robert special, philosophical look to avoid saying it sucks?"

"Kyle, would I do that," Robert laughed.

"'Bout five hundred words, OK?"

"Kinda short," Robert said, though secretly relieved. He could pound that out in minutes – though he first needed to read it.

"Yeah, I know, but here's part two," his friend replied. "I need you to go take a picture of the author tomorrow."

"Picture. Send one of your cubbies to do that," Robert said, referring to the myriad of young reporters Kyle seemed to always be mentoring.

"Can't. Too much in the hopper. Got a couple of guys on vacation and another tied up on a police investigation that looks newsworthy."

"Really. Excitement in our sleepy little town. What's the case?"

"You're not a reporter anymore, remember?"

"Well, you know how it goes; once a newshound, always a newshound."

"Yeah, yeah, yeah. It's a dead body that the police can't, or won't, say how it got dead, so we thought we'd help 'em out." Kyle chuckled, and added, "Anyway, just a quick picture; right downtown. Won't take a minute of your valuable time. I'll owe you lunch."

"Well, in that case, where will the lady ghostbuster be," he said, referring to the author, whose book, 'The Ghost You Need to Know', allegedly chronicled the other world must know personalities.

"Lora's place, on St. George."

"Mariner's Manor?" Robert asked, referring to the upscale nautical theme gift shop strategically located in the heart of the popular downtown part of St. George Street.

"Yeah, she's apparently doing something else on ghost stuff there. The editor thinks it'll be a good tie-in picture. That's why the review can be short and sweet, I need the room. Early afternoon," Kyle added.

"OK, I'm on it. I'll call you."

"Soon, Robert."

"Of course. It's top priority," Robert said as seriously as possible.

"Yeah, you're the essence of dedication and productivity. Bye."

Robert replaced the phone and mounted Bronco, reaching for a cigarette as he did so, a vice he had contemplated quitting many times. Not a heavy smoker, he had in fact gone without them for days on occasion, though he always returned to the nasty mistress, as he referred to them. He wasn't quite sure if he did so out of habit or companionship as he sat alone contemplating some scene in an article or story.

He should be more like Edmon de Valera in a story he once read. Arrested by British soldiers, he was being led off to jail when he took his beloved pipe from his mouth and smashed it to pieces on the walkway. His explanation to the soldiers was that rather than give them the pleasure of depriving him of smoking in jail, he just quit and, therefore, could not be deprived.

Returning the cigarette to its pack, he glanced at the unfinished article, then hit his computer lightly. It owns me, that beast, he thought. Always beckoning me to fill its screen with the great story, but offering no clue as to how to do it. Anyway, he needed to read the book and pound out the review—one week's rent, but he could feel a familiar beckoning, and as usual, he yielded to the call and headed the few blocks to his escape sanctuary, Louise's pub. Besides, he rationalized, a few minutes relaxation will make reading all the more easier.

Louise's was a tiny, ageless bar on the beaten path of the historic district, yet hardly noticeable because of its proximity to the old fort, city gates, and other prominent features. No food or ice cream, the choice of tourists, and an inconspicuous, hard to see sign brought few tourists inside. The few who did discover it usually lost interest when they discovered there was no jukebox or band and few seats, particularly on tournament nights, when local dart throwers showed up in mass. The situation was perfect for Robert because it fed his need to think and reflect; yet the faces of regulars gave him an inexplicable source of comfort.

Entering the small bar, he glanced around, waving to some of the regulars he knew. Spotting an empty stool and certain he could see his name on it, he moved in that direction, bumping the shoulder of someone in his haste. Turning, he saw a familiar, pale little man, perhaps fifty years old, sitting quietly, his hands cupped around a draft.

"I'm so sorry," he said to the bowtied gentleman. He had seen him in Louise's many times, never with anyone, but had no idea who he was.

That's what I like about this place, he thought, local color.

"Louise, let's have a mug," he said to the owner, telling himself one beer only, then to the book.

"Here you go, Robert. Don't spill it on the customers," she smiled, having seen him jostle the little man.

"Oh, the always witty Louise," he responded. "Don't give me another, even if I beg, I have work to do," he added.

"Robert, come on, we need a fourth," another patron yelled before Louise could answer.

"One game only, and I must take my leave," he quickly responded, selecting his weapon. I love this place, he thought, not for the first time.

CHAPTER 3

Robert shook his head, trying to dismantle the cob-webs and clear the ringing. The previous night's dart game had grown intense and the rematch challenge couldn't go unanswered. And, of course, everyone knows you can't play darts without beer.

Sitting up, he realized the ringing in his head was the phone.

"Hello!" He yelled, snatching at the receiver.

"Robert, hope I didn't wake you," the voice on the other end said, concerned.

Robert glanced at the clock. Six-thirty. A.M.!

"Clifford, it's six-thirty in the morning. That's when most people sleep. But in this case, I'm glad you called. I have some work to do." Robert took the edge off his voice, knowing Clifford had probably been up for hours, pulling crab traps, trotlines, and who knows what. "You at the marina?" he added.

"Yeah, had to get some gas so thought I'd give you a call. When you coming out?"

Clifford, the last of a breed, lived on the St. Johns River. No electricity, no phone. He was a lifelong friend of Robert's father and Robert and the most knowledgeable river-man in the area. Clifford's nearest connection to civilization was the phone at the marina two miles by river from his shack.

"Soon, Clifford. Just been busy. How you been doing."

"Oh, can't complain."   The old man gave his pre-dictable response.   Probably at least 80 years old, he really never did complain.   "How's that great American novel com-ing," Clifford added.

"Don't know, ain't found it yet," Robert answered the question Clifford had asked a hundred times.   It had become a long-standing tradition.

"Well, you will, you will," the old man chuckled.   Ever the optimist and proud as Robert's own father that he had done well writing, Clifford, an uneducated man had always encouraged Robert in his quest.

"Well, just thought I'd say hello."   Clifford paused. "Bass biting good," he added.

"And I'm gonna come out and catch some, Clifford. Soon."   Robert knew he needed to do just that.   He thought the world of the simple old man and enjoyed his company immeasurably.

"OK. Gonna hold you to it. Stay well."

"You too, Clifford." Robert responded to Clifford's stan-dard ending.   "I'm glad you called, Clifford. See you soon." He added, knowing the comment would mean a lot to the old man.

Robert replaced the receiver on the phone cradle and reached for a cigarette. He stared at the demon.

"I have fought in a war, endured a crazy woman, wrote sage, philosophical words, and still you perplex me."   Robert spoke aloud.

He remembered reading somewhere that it was more important to not want to smoke than to smoke.

The rub, of course, was that Robert was not sure he

had ever made that decision. Which is not to say he had not contemplated such a decision many times. The contemplation was enjoyable—mental gymnastics. The decision was not.

With pronounced movement, he replaced the cigarette and shut the flip top, proclaiming to the room, "Today, I am the master!"

That out of his system, he headed for the dependable, predictable, modern miracle that was his preset coffeepot, where the joy of morning would be awakened with that first, delightful sip.

He poured a cup, held it high and with a deep breath, stated, "To the book, all those ghosts I am about to meet and another opportunity to excel!"

Three hours and five cups later, the task done, he sat back and looked at his scrawled notes, barely legible. His father had once told him that his handwriting resembled a flock of heron's footprints left in the marsh mud at low tide. Probably, he thought, a good analogy. Anyway, he had a decent start to the review. Actually not a bad read, if you liked ghosts.

Realizing he was starved, he made another of his spontaneous decisions; the long way to Mariner's Manor, along the bay front, with a stop at his favorite breakfast eatery, then three doors down to the ghosts.

He checked his camera, threw on clothes, and headed out, not locking his door, a common habit, believing no one in their right mind would risk jail to break into a writer's house where at most the reward would only be an uncooperative computer and several sheets of wadded up paper.

As he approached the Bridge of Lions, so named for the lion statues which adorned it, he paused to observe the construction effort. The old bridge was getting a re-do, badly needed. He watched as the giant, hollow steel pipes that would eventually become the new cement pilings were pumped into place. As his growling stomach urged him onward, he wondered how much cement went into one of those monsters. Had to be tons, he thought.

Cutting across the plaza and turning onto St. George, he caught the smells pouring forth from his breakfast heaven—the Bunnery. His body started moving faster, thinking about the eggs, southern homefries, and fresh baked bread.

Ordering his feast, he sought a table, always hard to find at this favorite spot of locals and tourists alike. Others, some holding food, were searching about as well. As fate would have it, he passed a table as one of the seated patrons asked his tablemate if he was ready to go.

Robert stopped, his pre-planned strategy now implemented.

Moving quickly, he stepped to the side of the table, deftly cutting off the route of travel for others who might have the same idea.

"Oh, were you leaving?" he asked.

As a seasoned local, he knew this was not the place to be bashful if one wanted to sit. Besides, logically, everyone knows locals should have priority. It was an unwritten rule; a kind of payback for all those courteous directions patiently handed out to lost souls from far, far away.

"Sure, help yourself," the man responded.

Robert sat down as the couple moved out, noting a frown from two elderly ladies, laden with plates, also seeking a spot.

"Ladies, please join me," Robert quickly said, shoving dirty plates aside, knowing with a sigh of resignation the quiet breakfast he had hoped for would now be quite the opposite.

Sure enough, the now bubbly ladies sat down talking and never stopped. It is the curse of a local when a tourist realizes they have a goldmine of information before them.

Finishing his breakfast quicker than planned, he headed to Lora's.

"Robert, what a nice surprise!" Lora ran to Robert and embraced him in a giant bear hug.

"Are you playing tourist?" she asked, noting the camera dangling from his shoulder.

"No, I'm supposed to meet someone here— the ghost woman—and take her picture."

"Yes, Diane Eaton. I read her book. She isn't here yet." Lora responded.

"What is she doing here, anyway?" Robert asked.

"Why, Robert, we're haunted. Didn't you know that?" she replied mischievously. "She's working on something else and asked if she could prowl around the upstairs area. I think she's going to set up electronic equipment to listen in on those ghosts." Lora laughed, and added, "Come on to the back with me, I think my FedEx guy is here."

"Sure."

Robert followed her through the main store into a large stock room to a large steel and wood sliding door. She deftly pulled the old door back, its large, steel rollers shrieking in protest, to reveal a large loading dock fronting a small deadend alley.

Glancing down the open end of the alley, Robert noted one of the small public parking lots behind St. George Street.

"I grew up here and I never knew this alley existed," he exclaimed. I've gone right by it on Hypolita a thousand times," he added.

"It's a well kept secret," she laughed. "Free parking 'cause no one else notices either."

"I'll keep that in mind," he replied.

"Uh oh, knew I shouldn't have brought you back here," she said playfully.

"I promise I won't tell another soul. There's your truck," he added, pointing to the FedEx truck cautiously negotiating the narrow alleyway.

Signing for her delivery, she turned back to Robert. "Come on, I'll take you upstairs. Diane is probably here by now."

Robert followed her back through the storeroom, into the main shop and up the stairs to her art gallery. As she approached the back wall, Robert wondered exactly where they were headed. She reached the wall and opened a section, well camouflaged by faux painting. He followed her into yet another storeroom, right above the downstairs storeroom.

Rounding a corner, she headed up an old, rickety staircase into what apparently was a large, open attic. Robert hustled to keep up while he took in the old, weathered pine beams that crisscrossed the attic ceiling, their line broken every few feet by equally large vertical support trusses.

As they neared the top of the stairs, Robert could see two sets of ancient wooden block and tackle pulley systems dangling from a huge ceiling beam, much larger than the rest. He leaned over the top stair rail and realized he was looking down an elevator shaft—apparently hand operated. He could barely make out what appeared to be an old, wood and wire type door at the bottom.

"An elevator!" he exclaimed.

"No elevator. Just the shaft." Lora leaned over the top rail of the shaft and looked down. "I probably need to board this thing off. 'Course nobody ever comes up here. 'Cept Diane." She said, acknowledging the woman busy fussing with various pieces of equipment and wires.

"Diane, Robert Robson, one of St. Augustine's most eligible bachelors," Lora said playfully.

"Mr. Robson, what a pleasure. I read your books. They were wonderful." Diane held out her hand.

"Well, thank you, and I, yours," he responded, stepping across the partially covered board floor to take her hand.

Diane took his hand lightly, moving her other hand to join it in a two-hand greeting.

"Well, I'll leave you two alone," the ever mischievous Lora said. "I need to get back to the hoard," she added.

"Well," Robert said, freeing his hand, deciding against any further game of innuendo, "I just need to get a couple of pictures and you can get back to work."

"Of course, of course," she responded, with a tone of slight disappointment. She patted her hair into place.

"Where would you like to do it?" she smiled. "The picture, I mean," she added.

Oh, Robert, stay firm, he thought.

"How about a shot showing you setting up your equipment," he said. "And maybe a few questions for the picture caption," he added.

"Sure. I'll just start, and you shoot away."

After a few pictures covering all the bases, and the obligatory Q & A about what she was doing, Robert placed his camera back into the case and turned to leave.

"Well, very nice to meet you, Diane. I appreciate the time," he said.

"Oh, my pleasure, and it is I who should be thanking you for the review." She smiled, "At least I hope I should thank you," she added questionably, flashing a large, bright smile.

"Oh yes, your book is good. I think you'll be happy with the review," he responded, to ease her concern.

"Oh, wonderful! Please let me know if you need anything further. Anything, at all," she added, suggestively.

Feeling an urge to flee, he headed down, stumbling slightly on the piecemeal floor. He stooped to replace a small board over the twelve-inch deep space between two timbers. "Be careful of this shaft. Wouldn't be too hard to fall over," he said as he traversed the stairs."

"Thank you, I will," she replied.

Entering the store, Robert passed his longtime friend, busy with a customer, and waved. "Lora, you're incorrigible," he said, in reference to her comments upstairs.

"From what I hear, it is you who are incorrigible," she said with a laugh.

Without pausing, Lora turned to the group of ladies waiting patiently. "Ladies, Robert is one of our fine local authors. I have his books right over there and I know he would be delighted to sign a copy for you, if you're interested."

Robert shook his head at Lora's salesmanship and spent ten minutes describing his book to the impressed customers. Finally, extracting himself, he sprinted to the door with a final wave to Lora.

'NO LEADS IN DEATH INVESTIGATION', Robert read the Record's headlines as he passed a newspaper box. The drowning he recalled hearing about. Probably a tourist who failed to heed riptide warnings, he thought. No leads, the headline had stated. Wonder what that means, his former reporter mind wondered.   Drowning is drowning.   May be more to it.

He made a mental note to ask Kyle about it as he weaved his way through the now bustling mob of tourists on St. George Street, anxious to get back and put the review to bed so it would be ready for his friend.

CHAPTER 4

Robert stared at his half-burned cigarette.

"Your system is not a slave to a drug; you are a slave to a habit—major habit made up of a connected series of minor habits."

He realized he had spoken out loud. Where had he read that? Made sense. Kinda. Like now, he thought, sitting on the veranda, feet extended in the prop position to the railing. How can a fellow sit in this fresh air, relaxing, and not occupy himself with some mindless activity? It was like drinking beer at Louise's. Beer, cigarette, just goes together. Veranda. Cigarette. Relaxing. Cigarette. Seems logical.

Oh, well, he thought, glancing at his watch. Time to get outta here.

He grabbed the finished book review and pictures—good for one lunch—and headed off to meet Kyle at Café Aviles, a quaint little café they both enjoyed.

After the short, refreshing walk, he entered the small establishment to Nancy's usual greeting.

"Hey, writerman, missed good food, huh?" Nancy, the café owner was a personable single mom whose witty personality and unbelievable cooking skills brought locals into her place routinely. She enjoyed the luxury of not being dependent on tourist business as most other shops and restaurants were; a fact that no doubt accounted for her preferential treatment of the cracker crowd.

"Nancy, you know the answer is yes. You're the greatest," Robert answered her greeting.

"Yo, yo, yo." Kyle entered before Nancy could respond. "What's good, Nancy?" he added, sitting at a window table. "This OK, Rob?"

"Yeah, fine."

"This better be good since it's costing me lunch," Kyle said, taking the offered envelope.

As he glanced at the pictures to ensure scanning quality, a man entered and approached their table.

"Kyle, how are you?"

Then, as an afterthought, the man nodded at Robert and said simply, "Robert."

"Phillip," Robert responded.

Kyle looked from one man to the other and shook his head. In a small town, everyone knows everything, and Kyle, like most, knew of the two men's affection for the same woman and their mutual dislike for each other.

"Fine, Phillip. Join us," Kyle said, getting an 'oh, shit' look from Robert.

Phillip noted Robert's reaction, and with a slight smirk, took a seat across from him.

"Thanks, Kyle," Phillip said. "Hey, serving wench, beer," he shouted in Nancy's general direction.

"Coming up," she responded coolly.

Robert was not the only one who didn't particularly care for Phillip, and not just because of his fondness for Eve, the object of their mutual affection.

Phillip, in Robert's view, was a classic loser and parasite. They had known each other most of their lives, growing up in the small town and attending high school and college together, where Robert saw first hand Phillip's penchant for using people to get his way. After his old St. Augustine family, Minorcan descendants, had bought him into law school, they continued financing his life and bailing him out of his many sour deals and blunders. His reputation was that of a spoiled brat who drank too much and made empty promises.

"So, Phillip, the guy I assigned to follow-up the floating body tells me you're the executor. Did you know him?" Kyle said, breaking the uncomfortable silence.

"The archeologist? No, didn't know him. No family though so the court appointed an executor. In this case, I asked for it. Easy money," Phillip replied.

"Well, an ambulance chaser like you ought to know about easy money," Robert mumbled as he gazed at the menu. Making his lunch decision, he turned toward Kyle.

"I think I saw something about that in the paper. William something. Jumped from the bridge."

"William Stewart," Kyle responded between beer sips. "Actually, sounds like they surmise he jumped. Didn't find him for two days and he had scratches and bruises, but hard to tell how he got 'em," he added, looking at Phillip. "My guy says Stewart was a question mark; no family, no will, no friends that he could find. Said it seemed kinda strange."

"What's so strange? Probably a loser with no friends," Phillip answered.

Like you, Robert was thinking.

"So how do you resolve his property?" Kyle asked.

"Piece of cake," Phillip responded, "just put notice for claims in the paper, title search his house, then inventory and sell his stuff," he grinned, adding, "told you, easy money. Except, of course the inventory. He had a lot of artifacts. His house on Sanford Street is full of 'em." He drained his beer and waved for another. "Think I'll hire someone to do that," he added.

"I would think an expert like you would enjoy that experience," Robert said.

"Expert?" Kyle asked inquisitively.

"Oh yeah," Robert said. "Old Phillip here did a paper in college on St. Augustine history, and the many archeological finds." He looked at Phillip, "Unfortunately, he apparently didn't write a lot of it."

He was immediately sorry for his comment, knowing how childish it was.

"I wrote it. That asshole professor wouldn't believe me just because of similarities in a few books." Phillip spat out defensively. "I even showed him some of the family's old papers as my major research source. The jerk got excited about some of the old Minorcan stories." He glared at Robert, who started to add that Phillip had had a similar problem more than once in college, but decided there was no need to spoil lunch any further.

"Well, long time ago anyway," Robert finally said, to ease the situation.

"You should get Rob to do it. He's a man of leisure," Kyle threw in.

"What," Robert said, surprised.

"Do the inventory. Might be an article there," Kyle said by way of justification. "How much, Phillip?" he added.

"How much what?" Phillip, as surprised as Robert about this turn of events, responded.

"Money. How much money to do the inventory?

Freelancers always need money, particularly if they enjoy an active lifestyle. Right, Rob, boy," Kyle looked at Robert with a large grin.

"Very funny, asshole", Robert replied jokingly. "I simply enjoy participating in the joys life has to offer," he added.

"Four or five hundred bucks," Phillip said, looking at Robert. "But I doubt a world famous writer would be interested in crumbs," he added sarcastically.

Four hundred dollars, Robert digested, surprised, thinking of the boat repair bill he had just received.

"Well, I don't know. What else is involved?" he asked.

"Well, I, ah, you know, numbering, list, whatever. I'll get one of the clerks to do it."

Seeing Phillip's discomfort over the prospect of having him around, Robert looked at Kyle. "I could use a change anyway, Kyle. Good suggestion." He looked straight at Phillip, fidgeting in his seat. "So how 'bout it, Phillip, give me details, or do you need the money yourself?"

There was silence for a few seconds. Kyle took a big hunk of his shrimp burger, watching the verbal dance with a smile.

Suddenly, as if needing to answer the challenge, Phillip grabbed his pen and scribbled an address on a napkin. He fumbled in his jacket pocket, removed a key from a tagged ring and shoved both over to Robert.

"Knock yourself out. But I need it done in four days for an estate sale." He looked at Robert and added, "I'm sure I can tutor you through it."

Robert glanced down at the napkin and key, then took a long, slow drink of beer, his eyes never leaving Phillip's.

Kyle continued munching, enjoying the exchange.

Finally, dropping his stare, Phillip stood up and threw

money on the table.

"Well, I have better things to do." He said, giving Robert one last scornful look.

"Yeah, me too," Robert added, after the door slammed shut, knowing there was no way Phillip could hear. He looked at his friend.

"Well, that was real cute, Kyle."

"Hey, I was trying to help you pick up a few bucks," Kyle raised his arms defensively, pleading his case. "Besides, I was serious about a possible article. The guy was an archeologist you know. I'll have one of the boys do a little research." He looked at his friend.

"Is Eve actually still seeing him?" he asked.

Robert looked reflective.

"She's his nurturer," he finally said.

"His what?" Kyle asked confused.

"I think she feels sorry for the jerk. She's always looked out for his sorry ass, even when we were all growing up. It's like she feels sorry for him because he can't seem to keep a friend for long." He took another sip of beer and gazed out the window.

"Old habits are hard to break, I guess." Kyle finally said, breaking the silence.

Realizing Kyle had spoken, Robert turned from the window.

"I have more important matters to think about," he said. "Like fishing. When you want to go?" he asked Kyle.

"Good idea. I'm ready. Let's talk about it next weekend. Maybe try some reds in the intracoastal."

"OK. We'll talk. Let me know if you need anything else on the review," Robert said. "And by the way, thanks for the work."

"Will do." Kyle stood, "Back to the presses," he said, holding his hand out. "See you, buddy."

"You bet. Don't get caught in the rollers," Robert joked, taking his hand.

Deciding he may as well stop by Stewart's house to see what he had gotten himself into, he yelled goodbye to Nancy and headed down the street, pulling the address Phillip had scribbled from his pocket. Sanford Street. May as well swing by the Lightner and pay the parking ticket, he thought. One of the downsides to living in a tourist town—never enough parking spaces. If you needed to be somewhere and time was short, you parked where you could, and sometimes you had to pay the consequences. In this case, $7.50.

He strolled the small brick path lined with immaculately renovated old houses to cross Cordova where the Lightner museum and city offices were located.

"Let me guess, another visit to the fourth floor," a voice said from behind as he stepped onto the walk leading through the courtyard to the elevators.

"Gene, how are you?" he said, turning before he sighted the speaker. A city cop forever, Gene had one of those southern cracker voices that was both disarming and entertaining to hear. Robert had always been proud of his 'redneck' heritage. It took him a few years and maturity to realize that, but he was. There had even been a time, long ago, when some of his slow talking, drawling relatives embarrassed him with their speech. He had even been too self conscious of his own slangish vocabulary, often the source of an army buddy's joke during his stint with Uncle Sam. Now, he was embarrassed to remember being embarrassed, and enjoyed the uniqueness of the native north Florida drawl. Somehow, there was a totally unpretentious, genteel quality about it. Gene was a prime example.

"Well, you know how it is, gotta help keep you employed," he now added.

"I heard that," Gene responded, causing Robert to smile.

See, he thought, that's what I'm talking 'bout. Where else would 'I heard that' be understood in its proper context but here?

"Whatchyou got, a little ole' parking ticket?" Gene drawled.

"Yeah, and I think you might have written it 'cause a feller can't read it," he replied, unconsciously drawling more than usual himself. What was that saying, 'you can take the boy out of the south, but you can't take the south out of the boy."

"Lemme see."

Robert dug the ticket out and handed it to the old man, long ago relegated to the downtown beat handling the diplomacy type situations that usually involved tourists, though Robert knew his sage advice was often sought by younger cops.

"Naw, not me. Looks like that chubby little meter girl, Doreen," he said squinting at the ticket. "Tell you what, Robby, why don't I just make this thing go away," he said, using the childhood nickname Robert never cared for, though somehow, he didn't seem to mind Gene, or other old timers using it, as they always had.

"Now, I couldn't ask you to do that, Gene," knowing before it came what the response would be.

"Well, you sure cain't. That'd be illegal, but it ain't a big thing. We all got to take care of each other, don't you think?"

"I appreciate that, Gene."

"'Course, I wouldn't want to deprive you from seeing that little missy up on the fourth," Gene said, peering over his glasses at Robert.

"Gail and I just see each other occasionally, Gene. We're just friends."

"Hell, you could say that 'bout half the women in town." He smiled mischievously. "When you gonna settle on one? Like that pretty little thing over at the college. Eve, I think it is." Gene added, knowing exactly who she was but unable to resist adding a little melodrama to his teasing.

"Now, Gene you know that just wouldn't be fair to all them others," Robert replied, enjoying the little game Gene always played.

"Ha, ha, ha. I heard that," the old man said again.

Suddenly thinking about the archeologist, his writer's curiosity took over. "Say, Gene, that was something 'bout that feller they found in the bay. You know 'em?"

"That Stewart guy? Naw. Sounds like nobody knew 'em. Ole' Dudley said it's a real mystery." Gene said, referring to the head detective. "Tell you one thang, though," he added. "I don't think our boys buy that jumping from the bridge crap to do himself in. Hell, I've seen kids dive off that bridge." He peered at Robert. "Probably done it yourself the way you was," a big grin on his face. "Naw," he continued, "something fishy 'bout the whole deal. Man got no family, nobody much knows 'em, 'cept over at the college. Guess he did stuff over there sometimes."

"How old was he?" Robert asked.

"Well, best they could tell, looked 'bout your age. Been in the water three days though," he added. "Thing is, Dudley says some of them old women living by him over there on Sanford said he been there in that same house since they was young women." He smiled again. "I know some of 'em got to be 80, 85 years old." He shook his white head. "It's strange, alright."

Robert absorbed this information with interest.

"What about his house? Surely, there are records, for taxes and such." He asked.

"Well, you know City Hall. Dudley says that property records shows what looks like one of them pay back taxes and you own it deals though. Done by his same name, but way back in the early nineteen hundreds. Maybe his father. If it was, he never bothered to change it over 'cause ain't nothing else on it. Those old records kinda sketchy when you go way back."

"That's almost a hundred years ago, Gene. Had to be his father, or grandfather."

"No record of 'em!" Gene said

"Well, like you said, records get sketchy when you go way back."

"Yeah, sure is strange, though." He hitched his sagging equipment belt up. "Gotta go. See how many tourists are lost."

"Thanks again, Gene, I really appreciate your help with the ticket."

"Don't mean nuttin'. You take care, Robby."

"You too, Gene. Tell Irma hello for me."

"I will. See you soon."

Robert made his way through the courtyard and crossed Granada, turned down Cedar and made the jog across Martin Luther King to Sanford. He glanced at the address again as he walked, though he knew there were few houses on the little street, so it should be easy enough to

42

find.

He spotted the house on the other side of the street, so he turned to cross, walking around a horse carriage. The driver seemed to be looking in the direction of the house while he fiddled with the reins.

As Robert cleared the rear of the carriage, the driver glanced his way, then nodded.

He looks familiar, Robert thought. He watched the dark skinned man urge the horse forward at a quick pace. Looks Indian or maybe Spanish, he speculated, his memory offering no help as to why the man seemed familiar. But then, in a small town, everybody's familiar. With a shrug he turned his attention to the old hazardous looking steps of the house.

CHAPTER 5

Robert stepped onto the wrap-around porch of the turn of the century, middle class house. He reflected that he couldn't ever recall seeing an older house around here without a porch, the most important gathering place for southern folks in an era long ago. He noted the absence of any furniture or plants on the porch. Very unusual. Glancing up, he could see the old eyebolts that once held a swing.

Walking to his left, he followed the curve of the porch down the side of the small house, stopping at the rear steps that led into a small, fenced yard. The rear fence gate opened into a sort of unpaved resident turnaround, short cut, parking area, probably not designed for that use but evolving to that purpose.

He glanced through a window into the small kitchen, almost expecting to see a hand pump at the sink, which would probably have been part of the original décor. Turning, he retraced his steps to the front, fumbling for the key in his pocket as he went.

"You the police?"

Startled, he jerked his head up to see an old woman leaning over the adjoining fence with one arm, waving some unseen insect away with the other.

"No, mam," he replied with the expected greeting of southern gentility.

"Just have to do a little work here for a couple of days," he said, thinking he may as well let her know he'd be around more than once.

"They told me that feller done got himself dead."

Robert guessed her age at 80 to 85; hard to tell when a person reached a certain point. She wore thick glasses and seemed spry enough.

"He a friend of yourn?" she asked.

"No, mam, I didn't know him. Just hired to inventory the house," he added, to head off what would surely have been her next question concerning why he was there.

"No, didn't think so. Don't think he had any friends. Probably no family either. Unfriendly type."

"How long have you been here?" Robert asked.

"Been in this house almost 70 years. Came here as a young bride." She sighed. "My Gaston been gone almost fifteen years now. I shore miss that ole' fool sometimes."

"You've been here 70 years!" Robert said, somewhat surprised.

"That's right, almost 70 years. Born out on the river, but Gaston moved me here when we was married," she replied, filling in the blanks. "Ain't really changed that much 'round here. Lot of new stuff just outta town, though," she added.

"Yes, mam, we have grown some in 70 years."

He waited, not wanting to seem unfriendly, to see if the old gal had other thoughts on her mind.

Robert loved old people. Like most writers, he looked inside a person, almost unconsciously, always searching for who they were, what made them tick. He found the elderly usually had a lot to share. Their long lives, experiences and the trials of living to an old age, made them a wealth of knowledge, particularly about people, situations; the essence of living.

"How long did Mr. Stewart live here?" he finally asked, his curiosity compelling him to do so, and also because he usually found that older people enjoyed conversation. They were never in a hurry—sometimes a problem—but usually rewarding.

"He was here when I moved in," she stated matter-of-factly. "Don't know how long before that. He didn't like to talk. Traveled some, though. He'd disappear now and again. Off digging stuff my Gaston said."

Robert digested her statement. Gene had said Stewart was near his own age. Assuming he was a grown man when the old woman moved here, that would make him over . . .

"Some people like that, you know. Just like to keep to theirself. Nuttin' wrong with it, I guess. Probably had his reasons." Her voice had interrupted his calculations.

"I'm sorry. I didn't introduce myself. I'm Robert Robson," he said.

"Oh," she said patting her hair, "I'm Margaret Brown."

"Mrs. Brown. . ."

"Just call me Margie. Everybody does," she interrupted.

"Margie. Nice name." He searched for the right words, not wanting to offend Margie, then said, "If Mr. Stewart was here when you moved in, that would have made him awful old. Maybe it was his father here when you came."

Margie eyeballed him.

He hoped he hadn't hurt her feelings, the last thing he wanted to do.

"Well, Robert," she said knowingly, "I guess I can remember a man that lives next to me for 70 years. I ain't that bad off, yet," she added.

"Oh, no mam, I didn't mean . . ."

"That was another strange thing about him. He didn't seem to get much older," she cut him off.

"What do you mean?" he replied, telling himself Margie probably had a little memory problem. It had to be a relative of Stewart's here 70 years ago; not Stewart.

"Well, I mean just that. Man didn't age hardly none in all those years. Some, maybe, not much, though." Margie watched Robert's reaction, obviously enjoying the exchange.

"And the gentleman used to come see him all the time was the same way," she added, when Robert did not respond.

"But you said he didn't seem to have any friends," he finally said.

"I said hardly no friends. This one feller, skinny, mousy looking, nothing to 'em. Walked like an egret. He came a lot. Only one, though, and both of 'em always looked purty much the same all these years."

"Did you know his name?"

"Police asked me that too. No, never did. He was unfriendly like ole' Stewart." She looked reflective. "They both seemed educated men."

Again, Robert couldn't think how to respond.

"Maybe they found that Fountain of Youth," he finally said, jokingly.

She eyed him, squinting behind the thick glasses. "Robert, are you funning me?"

"Oh, no mam. Just a little joke."

She thought about this a second.

"Well, sense of humor is good, but I'm just telling you like it is." She then said in a forgiving tone.

"Margie, I think you're remarkable. I really enjoyed

our conversation. Maybe I'll see you again," he said turning back to the door.

"Always got a cake if you want to chat more."

"That's so kind of you. Maybe I'll take you up on that soon. Have a nice day." He wrestled with the old screen door as Margie's interesting revelation still swirled curiously in his head. She seemed very alert, he thought, but really old folks sometimes had memory problems. Getting back to reality, he turned to the task at hand.

Robert inserted the newly cut key into the dead bolt lock, which also appeared to be a recent addition. Maybe the police, he thought. Out of the corner of his eye, he saw that Margie was moving back to her own porch. He opened the door and stood still so his eyes could adjust to the dim light. The old, yellowed front window shade made a low clackety-clack sound as he raised it to get more light. The room smelled musty and inhaling, he noted the faint smell of pipe or cigar tobacco. His eyes moved slowly around the room. Small for a sitting room, as they were called in the past.

He moved about the room, making mental notes on the contents to decide how he should organize for the inventory. Not much furniture; two worn, overstuffed chairs, small table by the door and a large library type table. An old canvas bag and several artifacts, some in pieces, were scattered on its surface. He inspected some of the pieces. Most appeared to be of Spanish or Indian origin. Probably best to just number them as artifacts since he didn't have a clue what else to call them. More artifacts over the fireplace, but not much else, causing him to feel more comfortable about the job he had undertaken.

Moving to the next room, probably once a dining area, he noted an old roll-top desk complete with an old, slat back desk chair. Several bookcases lined the walls, some of the shelves displaying more artifacts, but mostly books and papers. He made a note to ask Phillip how to handle all the loose papers. He glanced into the kitchen. Standard items. A small eating table with two chairs. Entering a small hall-way, he peered into the first of what was obviously a two bedroom house. Couch, one large chair, and a coffee table, empty except for a pipe rack and several pipes. A fireplace appeared to have been used frequently. He passed a small bathroom and stepped into the main bedroom.

A large, ornately carved four poster bed took most of the space in what was obviously Stewart's bedroom. He picked up an empty glass from the small night table and sniffed. Good man, he mused, smelling the distinctive scotch whisky aroma, approving of Stewart's taste.

Placing the glass down, he moved to a large, standup chifferobe, almost identical to one his mother had. The draw-ers and door protected shelves contained the usual personal items. As he opened the last of the three small drawers, he smiled, recalling his mother fussing over what necklace to wear as she plundered through these same type drawers in her chifferobe. Stewart's third drawer held an old pocket watch, pocketknives, a broken pipe and a few tie pins and cuff links. He smiled again as he remembered, as a boy, his mother catching him plundering through her drawers, inspecting the contents. Then he recalled the false bottom in her drawer, where she kept letters and special items.

Robert carefully removed the watch and other items and pushed the drawer bottom slightly to the rear. It sprang open, revealing an old, worn, very thick book. He picked up the book, which appeared to be a diary or log of some kind. Guess I need to ask Phillip about this as well, he thought. He closed the bottom and replaced the items, deciding to keep the diary out until he could figure out what to do with it.

He went back down the hallway into the dining room— now apparently a workroom, and looked fondly at the old desk chair, thinking of his own Bronco. Impressive, he thought, settling into the comfortable and stable seat. Maybe I should buy this and retire Bronco, he pondered, deciding to ask Phillip if that would be appropriate since he was doing the inventory.

He opened the roll-top and immediately decided he wouldn't mind having the desk as well. Probably some rule against it, though. Placing the diary on the desk top, he reclined in the very comfortable chair and reached for a cigarette.

Robert shook his head, thinking, not for the first time that the most insidious thing about the smoking habit is that it gets all tied up with your other habits. Here I am, he pondered, relaxing in this fine chair, contemplating a plan, and my automatic response is to light up. The philosopher in him suggested that once he realized the true nature of these unholy unions, mixing normal habits with the smoking habit, and accepted that evil connection, deliverance would be at hand.

Sighing, he replaced the cigarette and picked up the diary, again noting its thickness. He opened the cover to the first page. The handwriting, obviously done with liquid ink, was small and more of a scrawl. Four or five lines and the date. Robert put on his reading glasses and squinted to make out the entry. Something about an upcoming job, dated . . . he held the book closer and focused. 1876.

1876! He looked again. Yeah, 1876.

Well, obviously this wasn't Stewart's diary.

Flipping through the pages, he could tell that the entries were not made on a daily basis, and not all were dated, as if done as an afterthought.

He flipped to the last entry and was surprised to see that it was made a few days earlier. Maybe Stewart took the diary over, he thought. He read the entry, not as faded, but in that same type scrawl, some words abbreviated:

We argued abt the vessel
again. He grows more insistent
that he shld keep it. . . .

Robert sat back and digested this situation. The entry was made just a few days ago, April 20th, and refers to an argument. Should he tell the police? Or Phillip? After all, the man's cause of death apparently had not been determined. And, he argued with someone. Maybe I should tell Gene about it, he thought.

Remembering that he was here to do an inventory and not an investigative report, he closed the diary and walked back to the front room. Glancing around one last time, he decided he had a plan for the inventory, which should not take long given the sparse furnishings and few personal items. He looked around again and retraced his steps through all the rooms.

"I knew there was something unusual here," he muttered aloud.

There were no personal or family pictures of any kind in the house. Two old paintings and a few pieces of old Spanish looking armor adorned the walls, but no personal pictures. A framed parchment looking document was mounted over a partially assembled suit of armor at the bedroom hallway entry. But no pictures. Maybe just an eccentric type, Robert thought as he decided to call it a day.

He took one last look around and headed for the

door, then stopped. Walking back into the study, he retrieved the diary, deciding it might be useful and, in any event, interesting to look through.

As he headed back toward the downtown area he decided a little exercise was in order and Louise's was about the right distance.

After the walk to Louise's and three drafts—because of the normal late afternoon shower which trapped him in the gathering place—he headed back home by way of the continuing Bridge of Lions construction. The huge steel poles being pumped in still fascinated him. He made a note to find out exactly how it all worked.

Entering his apartment, Robert hit his phone message machine and headed for his modest wet bar. His father checking in. Needed to call him. A magazine editor asking for a return call regarding a possible article. The usual telemarketer. Then Eve's soft voice saying she just happened to think about him and hoped all was well.

Securing his freshly mixed scotch and water, he hit his speed dial.

"Hello."

"Hi, Eve. Got your message. How's tricks?"

"Oh, you know, life in a small college where all matters are urgent," Eve said facetiously. "How are you, Robert?"

"Everything's good. Same-o, Same-o."

"Are you working on anything new?" she asked, knowing he was always playing with some kind of story.

Eve was one of the few people with whom he actually discussed details of works-in-progress. He had always been able to discuss anything with her.

"You know me. Always something in the hopper," he replied, deciding not to mention the inventory and Phillip, recalling that anytime his name entered their conversation, it created an uneasy atmosphere.

"I know you do," she laughed. "We should get together and catch up. Give me a call when your busy schedule permits." He knew she was teasing. A great sense of humor was one of the many things he really liked about her.

"I will. Matter of fact, let's plan on this week. I'll give you a ring."

"Good. I look forward to it. Take care of yourself."

"You too, Babe. 'Nite."

"Sleep tight, don't let the bedbugs bite," Eve replied using the childhood phrase Robert had heard many times before.

He hung up the phone and leaned back in his old chair, admiring the oil painting over his desk depicting an old Florida Indian scene Eve had given him years ago. Still his favorite. She had great taste. In more serious moments, he thought frequently of Eve and what she meant to him. Over the years his teenage aloofness had evolved to infatuation and finally to a genuine sense of caring. The relationship had grown somewhat serious on occasion, but there always seemed to be distractions. Both were independent, enjoying their lifestyles but also tentative about serious relationships because of a failed marriage for each of them.

And, of course, Phillip. Her nurturing attitude toward him and a refusal to accept what he was, had on many occasions ruined a good evening. But, Robert knew down deep that he really cared for her.

He sighed and studied the painting again; robust, tattooed Indians battling a huge alligator with sticks and bows.

He thought of Stewart's artifacts, wondering if any of those were Indian. Probably so. It would be interesting to find out what kind of archeological endeavors he had been involved in. Might even be some artifacts from the very tribe his painting depicted. . . the Timucua, Florida's earliest natives.

CHAPTER 6

Circa 1600

Florida was a changing land. There were still many independent Timucua tribes who never united politically, but were tied together by a common language or dialects of a common language. But their numbers were slowly decreasing, largely as a result of the Spanish invaders who early on had a propensity to wage war, and though there were now few skirmishes, they had also brought diseases the native Indians could not endure. Missionaries, colonists, and soldiers moved freely throughout the land, some living for periods of time with the "heathens." Horses were not uncommon, having been introduced by DeSoto many years before.

Nijo was killed by a cottonmouth moccasin, and his son, Antipola now presided as chief over the Utina. On his deathbed, Nijo had made his son renew his promise to guard the vessel, which had not touched human lips since Parucusi's death. Antipola was a fair, loyal man and had not forgotten his vow, having been reminded in many discussions by his father. There had been peace for many years, except for the occasional hunting ground skirmishes, or unfriendly encounters with the more ignorant soldiers.

The Spanish came and went in relative safety in Antipola's territory. He wished them no harm and had even befriended some, particularly Father Francisco Pareja, a missionary friar chartered to bring Christianity to the heathens. Father Pareja was also a linguist and recorded the many dialects spoken by the Timucua nation.   Antipola had enjoyed many discussions with his friend and missed him after he died less than one year ago.

Peace reigned, and though many Timucua, including Antipola, would have preferred the Spanish leave, the tribes, though growing ever smaller, continued their ways.   Now, Antipola had just received word that a new Spanish chief had arrived to take charge of the Spanish interests in this part of Florida. He greeted the news with passing curiosity, noting that many governors came and went. He joked about it with his son, Cacique, who would one day take the aging chief's place, though that was not automatic since the Utina, like most of the tribes were not bound by immediate lines of succession, so the chief's sister's son could become chief, and so on. More likely though, was that Cacique would inherit that position. To that end, he and his father had frequent discussions about many tribal matters, including the vessel. Though he lacked first hand experience with its consequences, Cacique was devoted to his father and the tribe, so he took each discussion seriously.

Governor Corcoles was, for the most part, a fair man. He took his charter to protect Spanish interests seriously but also respected the rights of the heathens and realized peaceful co-existence was necessary for both to thrive. On the job for only a few weeks, he was still in the process of being indoctrinated to the land and the people. At this moment, however, he was stiff and bored from pouring over the stack of papers on his desk, and the constant progression of visitors, all of whom seemed to either need something or desired to pass on their sage advice.

Stretching, he decided to stroll the compound. Passing the garrison chaplain's doorway, he noticed Friar Pareja's successor working inside.

"Oh, Father Pineda, how are you?"

"Governor Corcoles, how delightful, please come in," the smallish friar said, rising from his chair. "I hope you are settling in well, Governor," he added.

"Oh, yes. Well, lots to learn about the situation here, and the people, of course."

"Yes, yes, our heathen brothers are different, but we are spreading the faith."

"Yes, of course," responded the Governor, respectful of that mission, but content to leave it with the friar. "And do you know their ways and understand their language?" He asked.

"Well, some. Not as well as Father Pareja, but some." He patted a thick, leather bound book and added, "He was a linguist you know, and kept a wonderful journal that I find most useful."

"Oh, may I?" The Governor asked, reaching for the journal, not waiting for a response.

He opened the thick book and thumbed through the parchment pages.

"The father wrote with fine detail." He flipped through more pages. "Might I borrow it a few days? I think it would be quite helpful."

"Well, I, ah, I . . . ," the friar stumbled.

"Oh, come now, friar, I will care for it as if it were my own."

"Well, yes, yes, of course," the friar muttered, though obviously not pleased with relinquishing the journal.

"Wonderful, well, good day, then. I will have this returned in a very few days."

"Good day, Governor."

But many days passed, and still the journal did not return.

The Governor had discovered a wealth of information in the old book and had not even considered its return.

He was presently intrigued with entries based on Friar Pareja's time living with various Timucua tribes. They provided much insight into the heathens' lifestyle, their culture, beliefs and, he smiled, their myths. The current entry, like others, mentioned a chief Parucusi, who apparently went from a peace loving man to a ruthless warrior, attacking fellow tribes without provocation. And, the Governor could not help but smile again, all caused by a 'vessel', called tinaja, which bore the sign of an eagle feather, the Utina chief's mark. Seems this vessel, when drank from, not only extended one's life, but – the Governor scoffed – was evil, and changed the person for the worse.

Well, he thought, enough of this rubbish for tonight. Tomorrow, several Timucua chiefs were coming to call on him and he needed rest.

The next afternoon, the hot, July sun bore down on a very uncomfortable Governor, adorned in full, formal dress. The scene was almost humorous as the smartly dressed Governor being introduced to half naked savages.

As he went down the line of chiefs, each introduced by his interpreter, the friar, he appraised their looks. They were strong, muscled men, even though many were old. They were obviously proud, perhaps even a little defiant. He paused as the friar said chief Antipola's tribe. It sounded familiar. He bowed slightly, as he had done with the others, and surveyed the Utina chief. Similar dress as the others. Spear with feathers, a knife at one side and a leather pouch at the other. As he moved to the next chief, he glanced back toward Antipola, trying to recall why his name was familiar.

"Damn, is it always this hot?" The governor asked hours later as he entered his office. "Water, please," he added.

"Oh, yes sir. July is bad," responded Garcia, his aide, as he poured the water.

"I won't work long tonight, Garcia. Just want to look through the friar's journal again."

"Yes, Governor, I'll be right outside," Garcia responded.

The Governor opened the big journal about halfway and began slowly looking through its pages, stopping at one entry:

> I have received word that chief Parucusi
> has been killed in battle. Obviously,
> the myth is not totally accurate. The
> vessel does not keep one from dying,
> as the heathens would have you
> believe. Still, Parucusi was very old.
> Stories have him living the length of
> two men. His son, Nijo, took his
> father's vessel and promised peace.
> I pray this is true.

He continued flipping, then paused at another entry . . . a year later:

> Chief Nijo, son of Parucusi has died of
> snake bite. He was a well respected

chief among the other tribes. Some of
the chiefs are worried about what will
now happen. Antipola, the firstborn of
Nijo, is now chief and the superstitious
heathens, who long believed the vessel
was kept by Nijo in a pouch, but not
used, now fear its return. It is these beliefs
that I find so discouraging in my mission
work.

There! Antipola, that's why the name was familiar.
Fascinated, the Governor kept flipping, soon stopping at an
entry toward the end:

I have just returned after several
months with four of the larger
Timucua tribes. We are making
progress with the Lord's work,
but they are a superstitious people.
In my travels, I inquired when
opportunity permitted about the
vessel. I am amazed, and disappointed
at how many heathens, even chiefs,
believe its power to extend life.
Some don't like speaking of it
because they believe it is evil; hitiquiry.
Some say they saw it, with the
eagle mark of Parucusi engraved
on its side. Perhaps I should
find it and put holy water in it.

A sense of humor, the governor thought, smiling. He

turned the pages. Near the last entry:

> I have visited with chief Antipola for
> several days. I find him an hon-
> orable man, easy to converse with.
> I must confess my curiosity caused
> me to visit this particular tribe
> because stories of the vessel persist—
> even among our own soldiers.
> When I felt the time was right,
> I asked Chief Antipola if he believed
> the stories. I immediately regretted
> the question because the chief fell
> silent and stared at me. Shortly
> though, thank God, he simply said,
> "The tinaja killed my grandfather
> and many of our people. Now it
> is dead." I feared further questions,
> but I did notice as he answered, he
> had touched a leather pouch at
> his waist. Apparently, he has
> something and he, like the other Indians,
> believes it is bad. I cannot help
> but wonder if the chief, or others
> are tempted to test the powers
> of this vessel with a drink. Though
> I must add that the Timucua are
> very loyal and forbidden things are
> not done. This is a trait I greatly
> admire.

The Governor sat back intrigued. Chief Antipola had a

pouch at his waist. None of the others did. Was it the vessel? Pure superstition of course, its powers, but what was it? Well, it would make for grand parlor conversation back in Spain, he mused.

As the weeks and months passed, Governor Corcoles settled into his duties. There was much to do and his days were full. More colonists were coming to Florida and new garrisons had to be built and manned. The chaplain would inquire occasionally about the journal, obviously desiring its return, but Corcoles found it very useful. More and more as he read through the pages, he found himself re-reading the entries concerning the vessel. A logical man, given to dealing in facts, he could not accept the story as truth, but still, something about this vessel and its alleged power continued to occupy his thoughts. This increasing fascination and curiosity troubled him, even angered him on occasions, interrupting his work, as it was doing now. A knock at his door brought Corcoles back to the present.

"Yes," he yelled.

"Sir, the scout is here," his aide said as he opened the door.

"Senor Santos, please come in."

"You wanted to see me, Governor." Santos, not given to proper etiquette, walked in.

"Santos, you have lived among the heathens for many years. You understand them well, yes?" Corcoles asked.

"Well, good as any man can, I guess. They ain't so bad." The old scout, who came here some 40 years ago, replied.

Corcoles studied Santos, now relaxing in one of the large, ornate chairs. Finally he spoke again. "I wish to establish more garrisons west of St. Augustine. The friars will also operate missions from these garrisons to do the work of the church. The village of the Utina will be one such garrison." He paused to study Santos' reaction. Seeing none, he continued, "You have lived among the Utina?"

"Yes, many times."

"You know their chief?"

"Yes, Chief Antipola. Fine man."

"Do you think he would be receptive to such a garrison in his land?"

Santos straightened slightly and scratched his head. "I don't think so, Governor." He paused and continued, "He's friendly enough alright, but no, I don't think he would allow you to take over."

"And what of his son, Cacique?" The Governor asked.

"Well, don't really matter, he ain't chief," the confused Santos answered.

"Well, he's a young man. We been here since his birth so he's accustomed to our presence." He scratched his head again and added, "Different with the older heathens, though. They put up with us, but don't mean they like it."

"Ah, my thoughts exactly, Senor Santos. It would seem we could work better with younger chiefs. I wish to avoid conflict if that is possible, but the garrisons will be built in any event." The governor stood up and walked around his desk. He stopped in front of Santos.

"I wish you to go to the village of the Utina and request their chief to come to St. Augustine in seven days to discuss important matters with the Governor." He paused, then said, "Can you do that, Santos?"

"Sure, Governor, I been hanging 'round here too long anyhow."

"And, Santos, tell the chief he need not bring his entire

counsel, for I wish a private meeting."

"Well, the chief never travels without his counselor and a couple of warriors."

"But you will tell him none-the-less," the Governor insisted.

"Sure."

"Fine. In seven days, then," the Governor reminded Santos.

"Seven days," Santos repeated.

"Then I bid you goodnight and thank you for your service. You will be rewarded, of course."

"My pleasure, Governor. Goodnight." Santos said as he turned to leave.

"Santos." The Governor stopped the scout, who turned back.

"Forgive me, Santos, another question. You know the Utina chief well, do you not?"

"I guess so. Yes," Santos responded.

"Have you heard the story of this vessel object he is said to possess?" The Governor asked.

"Sure, tinaja. All the heathens know about it."

The Governor dropped his hands behind his back and paced about. "And do you believe their superstitious stories?" He asked.

"Well, them stories been around a long time. Might be something to it, might not." He paused and looked reflective. "I saw it, though," he said quietly.

The Governor froze.

"Yeah," Santos continued, "I walked by the chief's hut one day as he just finished making a new pouch. He took the vessel out of an old, torn pouch and put it in the new one."

"And how do you know it was the vessel of the stories?" The Governor asked.

"Saw the eagle feather, just like the stories say."

The men stood in silence.

"And does the chief drink from the vessel?" The Governor finally spoke.

"Oh, no, I don't think he'd ever do that. He guards it, as his father did. Them heathens believe the vessel is evil. It gives life, but puts a spell on the drinker." He paused. "No, I don't think any of them would drink from it."

The Governor felt suddenly anxious and dabbed perspiration from his brow with a handkerchief.

"Well, thank you again, Santos, seven days, then. And, Santos, I ask also that you remain in the chief's village until he returns from our meeting. Goodnight."

Santos left, shaking his head.

After he had shown the scout out, Garcia returned to see if Corcoles required his services any more tonight.

"Yes, Garcia, I have an important mission for you. I wish this to be kept out of garrison channels." He looked at his puzzled aide.

"Yes, Governor."

"In seven days, the Utina chief, with a small party will travel to St. Augustine. I want you to handpick a dozen men, swear them to secrecy, and kill the heathens before they reach here. Dispose of their bodies where they will not be found, Do you understand?"

"But, Governor, I do not understand. I thought we were to avoid conflict," the confused Garcia stammered.

"I know it seems unusual, Garcia, but I am concerned the Utina chief will attack us when we move the garrison in. Many would die. I am hopeful that his young son will be more receptive to our plans." He paused and placed his hand on Garcia's shoulder. "I do not like this method, my friend, but I do it to save lives. I know you must agree."

"Well, I, ah, I . .", Garcia caught himself, then said, "of course, my Governor, I will do it."

"Thank you, my old friend." He turned and strode behind his desk. "One more thing, the chief will have at his side a leather pouch containing an object. Please bring it to me. This is very important." He watched Garcia's reaction.

The aide did not fully understand this situation, but he did know the governor, and the power he wielded. While Garcia had long respected him, and was very loyal, he also knew that he had little choice in this current matter. He bowed curtly.

"Of course, my Governor, I understand. I will bring you the pouch," Garcia responded.

"Let no one else see it. Bring it only to me. When you have picked your men, give me their names." The Governor sat down as a sign of dismissal.

CHAPTER 7

Robert read the paragraph on his computer screen, decided the last sentence wasn't quite right and attacked the keyboard.

He regarded the keyboard as his adversary. The link between his thoughts and words on the screen. It was a game. If the cursor was blinking rather than moving, the enemy was winning. He sometimes would pound out a sentence he knew wasn't right in order to get into his attack mode, thinking that somehow the action may weaken the electronic beast's resolve and give him the high ground. One of the many games a writer sometimes played to maintain his sanity.

The last period appeared, the sign of the victor.

Hands clasped behind his head, he read the paragraph again. Picking up the smoldering cigarette from its resting place, he took a deep pull, coughed and crushed it out purposefully, noting the other three butts lounging in the large ashtray. Not bad. Four butts for one article.

It had taken him almost two days to gather information and complete the requested article, about a day longer than anticipated, thanks to a game of phone tag with the subject trying to set up an interview in Jacksonville.

Never enough time. He often took these jobs grudgingly, preferring to work on his own projects, but a buck was a buck. Deciding he would get back to his novel for a few days, he hit the print command and watched the laser printer marvel him with its electronic prowess.

The ringing phone jerked him back to reality. Deciding not to answer again—his normal habit when working—he glanced at the caller ID. Damn. Phillip; probably about the inventory.

"Hello," he said, deciding he should see what was on Phillip's mind.

"How's the inventory going?"

"Couple more days. I got hung up," Robert responded, reminding himself he really did need to get started. "There are lots of loose artifacts, so I thought I would just number them unless you can think of a better way," he added.

"Yeah, that's fine. Just keep it simple. No big deal. I know you're a busy boy," Phillip said sarcastically, then added, "don't screw around too long."

"You're such a charmer, Phillip."

There was a pause.

"I talked to Eve. Told her you were doing a little work for me. Said to tell you hello."

Good old Phillip. The master of the gloat. Always looking to twist the knife.

"Oh, well, that's nice, but I'll tell her myself when we get together this week," Robert replied, returning the favor, playing the game over Eve that had been going on since they were all much younger.

"I plan to spend tomorrow at Stewart's house, so I should be done soon," Robert finally added after getting no response.

"Discovered anything interesting yet?"

"No, not really much there, other than all those arti-facts. He apparently lived a very simple life." Robert replied. "By the way, did you contact any museums about the arti-facts? I'm sure they might be interested." He added, assum-ing Phillip had done just that.

"No, too much hassle. They can come to the sale like everyone else."

"Well, your call. I'll be through in a couple of days." Robert made a mental note to alert a few of the museums in town.

"Don't break anything." The phone clicked.

What an asshole. He thought again of the stupid infat-uation Eve had for the jerk. Just didn't make sense. She must be the only living person that doesn't see him for the loser he is. He replaced the phone, purposefully and gently, with a sigh of resignation.

There I go again, Robert laughed. Letting him get me agitated. He glanced at his watch. Too late to start anything else. Besides, Louise was beckoning.

Entering Louise's just before seven, Robert greeted a few regulars and looked around for a seat. The bar was full. Couple of people he didn't recognize, though one seemed familiar. Dark man, maybe Indian, nursing a beer. Robert noted tattoos on each arm as he passed, but couldn't make out what they were in the dim light.

He grabbed a small two-seater table as a young cou-ple departed. Louise showed up instantly with a cold mug in her hand.

"Now, how do you know I want a draft?" he asked playfully.

"Well, honey, if you didn't, it would be the first time in about twenty years!"

"Are you suggesting that I'm predictable?"

"No, writer-man, I'm suggesting you know it's two-for-one drafts for another hour," Louise responded with dramatic flair, hands on hips.

There was scattered applause around the room.

"To our favorite hostess, the great orator," Robert raised his glass to more laughter.

He took a big swig of the cold brew, feeling comfortable, as he always did in this place of merriment.

He took another sip, glancing at a new customer entering. The little, mousy man he had seen in here on occasion. The man removed his very out of date hat and glanced around looking for a seat. He spotted Robert, nodded, and continued his seat search. Funny fellow, Robert thought; walked in little choppy steps. The man approached the bar and stopped. He was staring at the Indian-looking fellow's back. Seemed nervous. Turning abruptly, he headed for Robert's table.

"May I join you?" he said in a soft voice.

"Sure, have a seat," Robert said somewhat surprised. He couldn't recall ever hearing the man speak.

"I'm Nathaniel Fuller," he said, taking a seat and placing his hat carefully on the table. "I see you in here frequently. Do you live nearby?" He glanced toward the Indian again.

"Robert Robson. Yes, I live a few blocks from here."

"Me too. I've seen you pass on occasion."

How strange Robert thought; all the times I've seen this man in here, and never a word, and now, Mr. Fuller seeks conversation.

Nathaniel proved to be quite an interesting conversationalist. Robert was impressed to discover he was a history professor at the small, private college in town and obviously passionate about his profession.

"I read one of your books, 'The Reckoning,' I believe. I found it quite interesting. You're a good writer," Fuller said.

"Well, that's very kind of you, but I'm sure as a history professor you have written far more than I."

"Oh, no, no, I've never published. Never seems to be enough time, and a great deal of reading is required in my profession." He sipped from his mug, then added, "I would like to write though. There's so much to choose from. I envy your ability to do it well enough to make it a profession."

Robert couldn't decide if he was being patronized or flattered.

"Well, Nathaniel, you know what they say, things are seldom as they appear. I take a lot of freelance jobs I'd rather avoid to hold down the gap between checks." He glanced at Fuller. "And, as I'm sure you will agree, time is a shrewd adversary and always seems to have the upper hand. Too bad the fountain down the street doesn't work; immortality, no time worries."

Robert had spoken in jest and was surprised at Fuller's reaction.

"What, what do you mean, immortality?"

"Fountain of Youth," Robert responded. "You know, eternal life, etcetera, that old Ponce never found."

"Oh, of course, how silly of me," Fuller stammered, regaining his composure. He glanced around the room, his gaze pausing on the Indian man's back.

"Well, I need a stretch," he finally said, adding, "would you care to join me on the walk home. I assume you live beyond me." He glanced nervously toward the Indian again.

Robert glanced at his watch, "Wow, almost ten. Guess I lost track of time." He stood and unkinked his back. "Sure,

I'll join you. We can continue our talk," he said, realizing he had truly enjoyed their time.

"Excellent," Fuller replied, gingerly retrieving his interesting hat from its resting place.

Their small talk continued as they strolled down San Marco toward Marine Street. Mostly mundane things, though Robert did reveal a few personal tidbits, sharing in that strange way strangers will often do. Things not readily volunteered to friends. He found the little man very easy to talk with, though he would realize later that Fuller had actually revealed very little about his own personal life.

As they turned onto Cadiz street, Fuller glanced over his shoulder down the dark street as he had done a few times during their walk. Robert took a quick glance as well. A couple sitting on a brick wall, and a lone figure walking further back. Nothing unusual for a tourist town at night.

"Well, here I am," Fuller stopped in front of his cottage-size house, again glancing around.

Robert followed his gaze and again saw the lone figure, who had also turned on this street. Again, not unusual, but Fuller seemed so nervous, almost paranoid, Robert thought, remembering how over watchful he had been in the pub.

"Would you care to come in for a nightcap before continuing your walk home?"

Another surprise. An invitation into the home of this private little man. Fuller was fumbling for his key, still looking down the street, as if he were being watched. Finally retrieving the key from a vest pocket, he glanced up quickly, his small, dark eyes darting about.

"Oh, here we are," he said, turning to the door.

Robert was not sure what to do.

"I don't want to impose, Nathaniel. It is getting late," he managed to respond.

"Please, a quick drink. I've really enjoyed our time together," Nathaniel replied, almost pleading.

Now faced with a small dilemma—Robert was curious about Fuller, but wasn't really looking for a new buddy—he glanced at his watch. Why not, he decided. Besides he needed to visit the bathroom.

"Sure, a quick drink."

Fuller opened the door and turned on the hall light, standing aside for Robert to enter.

CHAPTER 8

Robert stepped into the ancient looking room, filled with turn of the century furniture, including a beautiful old oak library table filled with newspaper, magazines and books. Conquistador type helmets and weapons adorned the walls and rock fireplace mantle.

"May I use your facilities?"

"Certainly. Right through there on the left," Fuller pointed to an opening.

Robert closed the bathroom door and looked around. He was, he thought philosophically, like most people, always curious about a new acquaintance's bathroom. It was, after all a personal place and could reveal much. An old, modest vanity shelf held the usual items, and he was not surprised to see an old, well-used shaving mug, brush and straight razor. He smiled, thinking it matched Nathaniel's dress code. The little man seemed to have a fondness for the past. A well worn leather sharpening strap hung from the wall, attached to an equally ancient brass hook. An electric toothbrush seemed out of place among the iron claw bathtub and chipped, pedestal style sink.

As he was toweling his hands, he decided to complete his curiosity inspection and opened the small, age clouded mirror door. The shelves were almost bare. Not even a pill bottle. Strange, he thought, Nathaniel sure doesn't look that healthy. Must be living right.

Different kind of man, he thought again, finishing the business at hand.

"You mentioned you enjoyed scotch whiskey, so I took the liberty," Nathaniel said as Robert entered the living room.

"Oh, good stuff," Robert said, sniffing the offered glass.

He glanced at the bottle of very old scotch.

"Now that's smooth scotch," he added, taking a slow, deliberate drink.

"Good, I'm glad you find it worthwhile." Nathaniel poured a small portion into his own glass.

"I'll join you."

"You have a very comfortable place. Have you lived here very long?"

"Yes, quite a long time," Fuller laughed.

"But then, time is relevant, like most things." He added.

"Well, that's definitely true. And never enough of it. The one thing beyond our control," Robert added.

Nathaniel's eyes twinkled mischievously. "Yes, I guess that's true, for most things," he said.

Robert studied the curious little man. He guessed his age at about sixty. Thin and awkward looking, yet youthful somehow.

"So tell me, Robert, are you working on a book now?"

"Oh," Robert stammered, realizing he had been staring, "always something. Nothing overwhelming, I'm afraid."

"Oh, I'd love to hear about it."

There are interesting differences in every writer's work process. Some prefer to isolate their thoughts about a project. Think through scenarios. A secretive process to get a plot, or character, or twist, set, not wanting to share the methodology with others. Perhaps a fear that other input may complicate or clutter the maze of possibilities. Others prefer, and even need verbal interaction to 'wargame' an idea, get reactions as the project proceeds. For the most part, Robert fell into the former category. Usually preferring the loner style. With few exceptions, Eve for one, he usually didn't discuss his on-going work. Somehow, though, Nathaniel seemed so interested and easy to talk to. He had, throughout the evening, found himself sharing his ideas, glitches, and surprisingly, discovered Nathaniel's insight was very helpful. Not unlike Robert's friend, Clifford, whose eighty years of life's experiences made him very wise. Fuller, likewise, seemed very savvy for a man only a few years older than Robert.

"Well, I've been yakking far too much," Robert now said, realizing he had gotten caught up in his explanation of a story problem and had been talking several minutes.

"Oh, nonsense. I find it fascinating." Nathaniel quieted his concern.

"Nathaniel, I noticed some of these newspapers and magazines are really old. Are you a collector?" Robert said, trying to shift the conversation to Nathaniel and his interests.

"Not really, but as a student of history, I find it interesting to see history as it was originally captured, rather than excerpted in a book years after the fact where too many so-called historians allow their own opinions and perspective to change the actual event; or worse, they change it purposefully so it will fit their own theory or opinion of how history happened."

Robert detected a slight scornful tone in Nathaniel's voice.

"But where do you get them?"

"Well, most I purchased from newsstands at the time," he seemed to catch himself. "Of course, there are places you can get old articles," he finished, somewhat defensively.

"But these seem to be originals."

Robert moved a paper from the pile, noting the date. "And this one's over a hundred years old."

"I love history, so I managed to get things here and there; papers, old artifacts," he said, gesturing around. "There are always things around. One just has to be patient. It takes time."

"Yeah, I suppose when you study history, time really does seem relative. Our lives are a mere dot on the page of history." Robert sipped his scotch.

"Yes, the study of history is very time consuming. So much to read, research, discover. Too much for one lifetime." Nathaniel gazed thoughtfully at his drink, eyes twinkling, as though he were reflecting on some humorous secret. "One needs so much time," he continued softly.

"Well, I need to visit the facilities this time," Nathaniel said, snapping out of his trance. "Excuse me a moment."

Nathaniel scurried toward the bathroom. Robert stood and stretched, realizing he had been there over an hour. He walked around the room, stretching his cramped legs, admiring the various artifacts as he wandered aimlessly.

Nathaniel's décor reminded him of Stewart's house. Very modestly furnished with old furniture. Few amenities; actually no amenities. While the house was very neat and orderly, the walls obviously had not been painted in years. They were not really dirty, but the years had changed what was probably once a flat off-white to more of a grayish hue. Old style spring-loaded blinds, more yellow than their original white, served as curtains. They were all pulled down, positioned three or four inches from the window sills. A beautiful wall clock was positioned over the small fireplace. Apparently very old, the face of the clock was yellowed. A glance through the face glass revealed two brass keys used for winding and setting the time.

He picked up a curious looking object from a small, box-like base and examined it. Maybe Indian, he thought. Setting it back carefully, he noticed the intricate carving on the small base. Curious, he ran his fingers over the carved design, tracing an almost calligraphy like line across its side. The discreetly indented wood was perfectly smooth to his touch. Suddenly, the front of the box fell open. Holy shit! I broke it, he thought. Then he looked at the etched line and saw a tiny release mechanism, hardly noticeable, which obviously opened the front, like a secret compartment. He looked into the box end and saw that it contained a small, almost jar-like object; perhaps some kind of drinking glass. Bending to get a better look, he could see a design, well worn, etched into the surface. Maybe a leaf. Or a slender flower.

Robert fumbled for his glasses to have a better look, but in his haste, they fell to the floor.

The commode flushed. He quickly retrieved his glasses, closed the box lid and headed back to his seat but had only gotten halfway when Nathaniel re-entered.

"Stretching my legs." Robert offered, hoping the lame explanation would sound legitimate.

Nathaniel stopped. He stared at Robert then glanced toward the box, his manner suspicious.

Shit, Robert thought, he probably thinks I'm a snoop—which I am.

"This has been most delightful," Robert finally said, taking his seat again, thinking he shouldn't just run off like a thief in the night.

"Yes." Nathaniel paused, watching Robert. "I have enjoyed it as well." He fidgeted with his glass.

"Did you discover anything of interest? I could fill in the background for you." Nathaniel's offer, and challenge, was delivered in more a scolding than helpful tone.

"You really have collected many quite interesting antiques and artifacts. I am particularly impressed with the wall clock. It must be terribly old." Robert finally collected his thoughts and responded.

"Yes, it is very old. It was a gift from someone very close many years ago." Nathaniel replied in a monotone voice.

The mood had changed. Robert suddenly felt like an intruder. The relaxed comfort level they had enjoyed throughout the evening had shifted to one of uneasiness, as if he had violated Nathaniel's confidence. He seemed such a private person, anyway. Probably seldom, if ever, shared his thoughts with others as he had done with Robert.

Robert took a sip of the smooth scotch, desperately searching for a way to relieve the tension.

They both became uneasy and Robert's gracious attempt to talk of other things was strained. After Nathaniel had glanced toward the box a second time, Robert stood and thanked him for the evening. They were both relieved as Nathaniel opened the door, again glancing down the street as he showed Robert out.

Nathaniel offered his hand almost tentatively.

"Thank you again for a wonderful evening," Robert said, taking the little man's hand loosely in his own.

Nathaniel nodded without responding and turned away.

As the door shut, Robert stood for a moment, somehow feeling like a kid that had been caught with his hand in the cookie jar. Though he and Nathaniel were not close friends—hardly knew each other really—something had quickly developed between them.

And now it was different.

A crude type of one night stand, sharing things, then a realization that much had been revealed. Now, it felt as if a veil of suspicion had been dropped; a questioning of motives and consequences. He felt awkward, almost embarrassed, that he had talked of things with Nathaniel that he seldom revealed to others, except perhaps Eve, and he felt Nathaniel had done likewise, but now almost certainly regarded him in a different light. Robert felt a rollercoaster of emotions; traitor, snoop, confidence breaker. But, most of all he felt anger at himself.

He lit a cigarette, with no philosophical thought about the smoldering demon in his hand. He thought again of Eve, suddenly wishing it had been her he had been sharing his thoughts with. Thinking of Eve made him feel better. Smiling, he recalled the first time he had consciously realized his true feelings for Eve, many years ago.

It was a few months after his divorce from a marriage that lasted six years and had been a mistake from the beginning. Eve's own marriage had failed two years before.

Robert had just returned from an out of town trip required for a magazine article he was writing. The trip convinced him the article was all wrong and would need a new slant. He needed to clear his head so he dropped into a local nightclub, looking for a remedy to soothe his aching head and demoralized attitude. Eve, always a music lover and dancer, was there.

Robert and Eve's mutual friends had always teased her about her aspiration to dance professionally, which she would never confirm or deny. The truth was she just loved to dance. Robert had been her escort in both high school and college at many dances, though she seldom confined herself to one partner, since most young men were limited to certain dances; not so good at others. Robert had not been an exception, and Eve had no limitations, many times never leaving the floor as different styles were played and new partners materialized. It was not a cause for jealousy, if one knew her. Eve just loved to dance and often came and left alone.

So, on that night as he entered the club, he was not surprised, but was delighted to see Eve dancing effortlessly to the heavy beat booming from very large speakers positioned throughout the upscale club. He smiled, noting several men dancing around her, though probably none had been invited. Their movements varied, from the wild to the more subtle, 'I'm different' style, all obviously seeking to catch her attention, but as Robert could have informed them, she was immune to their gyrations. She was totally consumed by the music.

He watched her move among the uninvited, would-be suitors. She was gorgeous, but not in the centerfold model sense. A classic type of beauty. Tall, probably five-nine, though appearing even taller because of the unusually high, tight bun — her 'dancing do' — as she called it, formed by her long, silky, light brown hair. Her face, not beautiful, but perfectly formed was highlighted by large, blue eyes, high cheekbones, and full, pink lips. Her light, long dress veed deeply into firm, well-formed breasts. Her beautiful, olive skin, tanned slightly from long beach swims, a testament to her flat stomach.

There were many beautiful women in the club, but she was the one being watched with the most admiration. The men watched her every move. Some pointed and playfully shoved each other because they knew they didn't have a chance. Others, more seasoned and calculating, hung back scheming a plan. Still others, stupidly, tried to take her over.

Robert, ever the philosopher, knew it was not her unique physical beauty that attracted men. It was her entire demeanor, the way she carried herself. Eyes closed, she never danced too quickly or too slowly, but always in perfect harmony with the music. As though the instrument and words were making love to her. She was oblivious to the men about her, even as new suitors appeared and others faded into the mass looking for easier targets, finally giving up on Eve. Robert was mesmerized, watching this creature sway rhythmically

He positioned himself closer, never taking his eyes from her. He suddenly saw her differently and he was too struck to worry about pride. He stood as much in the open as possible, hoping she would acknowledge him. He thought he caught a look, but knew it was probably his hopeful imagination. He finally turned and headed to the bar, shaking himself back to reality. Then she was there, saying his name and pulling him onto the dance floor, shredding what little hope the remaining suitors may have had. They had danced and laughed for hours, finally collapsing in her apartment.

The memory made Robert smile as he realized he had walked past his apartment. He retraced his path and stepped inside, feeling suddenly alone. Without thinking, he reached for the phone.

"Hello."

"Eve . . . I hope I didn't wake you," he said, realizing how late it was.

"Robert, you can always wake me. Besides I was reading, just being lazy."

"Well, I ah, I was just thinking about you and thought I'd call." Damn! Sounds like a high school kid, he thought.

"Is everything alright?" Eve asked, a worried tone in her voice.

"Oh, yeah, everything's fine, I just . . . ," his voice trailed off.

"Look, I'm sorry. I shouldn't have called this late. I'll talk to you tomorrow."

"Robert," she said teasingly, "has someone been drinking a little?"

"No, no. Well, yes, but only a little," he replied defensively. "Eve, I'm not drunk!" he added.

She laughed.

"Robert, I know that. You never get drunk. That's one of the many traits I like about you."

Embarrassed now, he let out a long sigh.

"Was there something on your mind, Robert?" she asked after a pause.

Somewhat regrouping, he cleared his throat, trying to regain his stoic demeanor. "No, Babe, just being silly and a little melancholy, I guess."

"And you thought of little ole' me," she teased.

"Well, your phone number was handy," he replied, getting into their normal easy conversation mode.

"I'm so touched," she laughed.

"Besides," he continued the game, "I said I'd call you, so I thought I'd go ahead and get that chore out of the way," he finished in the most aloof voice he could conjure up.

There was a long pause.

"Robert."

"Yes, Eve," he replied waiting for the next playful barb, already preparing a response.

"You said we'd get together this week," she said in a husky, half sleepy voice.

"So I did. What's good for you?"

"Now."

"Now?"

"Yes. Grab your toothbrush."

He pictured her propped up in bed and felt slightly lightheaded.

"Ten minutes?" Robert managed to say through the big grin that suddenly adorned his face.

"I'll unlock the door."

CHAPTER 9

"I'm glad you called." Eve poked Robert's ribs playfully, then added, "And what does the great philosopher make of this evening's turn of events?"

He kissed her forehead.

"Two lost ships in the night, docking again in a safe harbor," he replied in a dramatic voice.

Eve ran her fingers along his chest as they lay together watching the candle flicker beside them.

"I see you still do the candle thing," he said, knowing her habit of always lighting a candle before any of their romantic encounters.

"Only for my great author," she mumbled.

"Truly?" He rose to a sitting position.

She sat up, not bothering to pull the sheet around her bare breasts.

"Yes, Robert, truly. It's reserved for my special beau."

He studied her face, searching for the usual mischief, but saw something else.

"Well, I think it's wonderful," he finally said, clearing his throat.

She clasped both hands around his neck and kissed him deeply.

"So you haven't told me what you're working on," she said, releasing his head and pulling his arm around her neck as she pulled them both down on the bed.

"Oh, you know, this and that. A new novel, but haven't really got it going yet. I'm spending far too much time on freelance stuff. It's another of life's dilemmas; sometimes they create a good change and clear my head. That's how I make myself feel better about doing them. Other times they are more of a chore that has to be dealt with." He looked at her. "Even famous authors like to eat, you know."

He let out a long sigh, wishing he could light a cigarette, but he knew Eve viewed smoking as a disgusting habit and a lecture would surely ensue.

Another routine habit-smoking link. Sex and smoking. Visions of smoky, blue clouds spiraling upward, over contented bodies. The aroma mixing with the sexy smell of perspiring bodies, the haze enhancing the relaxed mood. What a fit! But delusions all! Reality was coughing from the smoke, the terrible after taste to be shared with the happy expectancy of a sweet kiss for your partner, who no doubt grimaces over the breath sweet as mignonette. It all sounds so logical.

His philosophical meandering was interrupted by Eve's sleepy voice.

"Phillip said you were working for him. That's a change."

"I'm not working for Phillip!" he responded defiantly.

He rose from the bed and strode to the open window, enjoying the gentle breeze blowing through.

"Well, don't get so cross. I just thought it unusual," she said apologetically.

He suddenly felt angry.

He turned, standing naked, to face her in the dim light.

"What is it with you and that jerk, anyway," he demanded.

"There's nothing with us. He's just a friend, you know that."

"I know he's an asshole."

"Why have you always disliked Phillip so?"

"I haven't always disliked him. Only since I realized he's an asshole!"

Getting no response, he continued.

"He's a drunk and a user. He uses people. Always has, since we were all kids." He paused, then added, "Just like he uses you. You're probably the only friend the fool has." He gestured helplessly. "I just don't see what someone like you sees in him."

"And what is someone like me?"

He turned back to the window.

"I mean, you're just a neat gal. There are a ton of men that would kill to hook up with you, but you choose to nurture the town jerk." His voice had softened as he calmed his demeanor, realizing this was old ground.

"What about you?" she asked softly.

"What about me?"

She rose from the bed and moved to the window, wrapping her arms around his torso. Her face felt smooth against his bare back.

"Robert, Phillip is just a friend. And you're right, he is different, and he doesn't have many friends."

"Many! He doesn't have any!" He felt his body relax even more as she pressed her firm breasts against him. "Did it ever occur to you why that is?" He added, realizing the conversation was headed into deeper territory than their discussions had in the past. He didn't care. He just hated the thought of Eve and Phillip having any kind of relationship.

"Yes. I admit it. I feel a little sorry for him. I know

he can be deceitful and irresponsible, but it doesn't hurt to give him a little compassion. Everyone deserves that."

That was Eve—rescuer of stray cats, collection coordinator for those in need. So naïve sometimes.

"Robert," she forced him to turn around and stared into his eyes. God, she was beautiful, he thought, growing even more calm. He found it difficult to think as he gazed at her tanned body, accentuated by the moonlight filtering through the window.

"Phillip is a friend. We all go back many years. He's just a friend." She took his face, then continued, "You're more than a friend. Surely you know that."

He returned her stare, stunned. There. One of them finally said it. Maybe his feelings weren't so one-sided after all, as he had always assumed—or feared.

He took her in his arms. "I'm so glad, Eve, because you're very special to me. I think you always have been."

She pulled away, eyes glistening with tears.

"I'm glad." She gave him a peck. "Shall we change the subject?" she asked again playfully.

"No. You're right and I'm being childish." He grinned at her. "Teenage jealousy. It's the way big boys are, you know. We never seem to grow up in that department." He added.

"Well, you have absolutely no reason to be jealous." She touched his face with a warm hand. "You don't realize what a cool dude you are." She said, using the college jargon. "You're in like flint, and I'm glad it's mutual."

"Anyway, I'm inventorying a dead man's house for you-know-who, and it was Kyle's bright idea. Pays good, though," he said, deciding to act like a big boy.

"A dead man's house!"

"Yeah, you know, the guy they fished out of the bay."

"Stewart, the archaeologist?"

"The same."

"That was terrible." She climbed back in bed. "I saw him at the college several times. He did occasional lectures."

"Really." He pondered this a moment, then added, "What do you know about him?"

"Well, nothing really. Seemed to keep to himself. Not very talkative."

"How long has he been working at the college?"

"Well, I don't think he ever worked there. Just occasional lectures, workshops; that sort of thing. You know, like a visiting professor." She thought a moment. "But I've been there over twenty years and he was there when I arrived. I can't believe that much time has passed. Anyway, I think he had been there for quite a long time when I started."

She looked reflective.

"As a matter of fact, I did hear old Mrs. Dempsey, the librarian, recall an incident that happened her first year there that involved Stewart, and she's been there over forty years."

"What kind of incident?"

"I don't really know. I think he got into a big argument with the college president about some kind of research project he was involved in."

Robert stood, staring out the window.

"Why all the interest? Come back to bed."

"Well, it's just curious. There's hardly anything in his house. Bunch of old artifacts, no pictures at all. And his house is a throw back to another century."

"That is strange." She paused. "I think he was kind of an expert on early Indian things so maybe he was the work obsessive type, no time for families. He and little old

Professor Fuller did research together over the years." She touched her lips with a finger in thoughtful gesture. "Come to think of it, I seem to recall Mrs. Dempsey mentioning Professor Fuller being involved in the argument somehow. I really can't remember, though." She added.

Robert turned from the window.

"Nathaniel Fuller?"

"Yes, do you know him?"

"No. Well, kinda," he walked to the bed. "I've seen him often, but we really just met recently," Robert responded, deciding to skip any discussion of his earlier evening activities.

"But, you say they knew each other?"

"That's right, at least academically."

Robert digested the information, recalling one of Stewart's diary entries referring to someone by the initial N. Surely, it couldn't be Fuller.

"How long has Fuller been at the college?"

"Forever." Eve responded, matter-of-factly.

"What do you mean, forever?"

"It's a joke. No one remembers when he came," she laughed. "To hear Mrs. Dempsey tell it, he was born there," she added.

Well, this was all very interesting, Robert thought. Was this just a case of two old eccentric men befriending each other? Is Fuller the N in the diary?

"Robert."

Eve's voice startled him from his thoughts.

"Why are you so curious? You and Phillip," she added.

"Phillip?"

"Yes, Phillip was quizzing me about Professor Fuller too. What's the big interest?"

"What was he asking?" Robert asked, his curiosity even more aroused.

"Well, everything. Just like you." She gave him a quizzical stare. "What's going on? Why all the interest in an old professor?"

Robert turned and faced the window again.

"Well, this obviously has something to do with Stewart's death. Why all the curiosity; and mystery?" She prodded, when Robert did not answer.

"Robert?"

"Oh, sorry, Babe. Just thinking." He responded, turning from the window.

"Well, since you are so preoccupied with this matter, I can tell you that Stewart did know Mr. Pena."

"Phillip's father?"

"Yes. I remember several years ago he came to the college to pick up something Stewart had said he would leave for him. No one knew anything about it, so Mister Pena explained Stewart had borrowed some old family letters and papers and he just wanted to ensure their safe return. We told him we would pass on his message, and that was the end of it."

"What kind of papers?" Robert quizzed.

"I told you, family things. That's all I know. You know they are Minorcan and go way back. I'm sure it was just a research related thing."

"Did you have other questions, sir, or can we relax now." She added, with a flair of melodrama like a suspect being interrogated.

Robert smiled crookedly, realizing it all must sound Sherlock Holmesish. "No more questions. Just writer's curiosity. You know how we are."

"And, Phillip? He isn't a writer. Why is he also so curious about everything?"

"Phillip is probably trying to find a buck somewhere." He laughed, trying to make light of the discussion.

He sat on the bed and took her face in his hands.

"Eve, this was wonderful, but I have to go." He couldn't take his mind off Stewart's diary.

"It's one-thirty in the morning," Eve said, glancing at her clock. "Besides, I had some other plans," she added with a sexy smile.

He gazed at her long, slender body, still uncovered. What were you thinking! He felt his old investigative reporter urges yielding to the situation at hand. How could a sane man leave this for two old men and an old, beat up book?

"Show me," he grinned mischievously.

Without words, she pulled him onto the bed and straddled his waist, penning his arms.

"Surrender yourself to my care, ole' great author." She bent to him before he could respond.

Robert had visions of Phillip kissing her like she was now kissing him. As he quickly surrendered to her passion, and his, those thoughts evaporated like the dampness of a street under the Florida sun. Not possible, his logic concluded.

CHAPTER 10

Phillip sped through the quiet streets of early morning St. Augustine. Unable to sleep, a common occurrence, he had finally decided to go to his office to do paperwork, his usual pounding hangover adding to his malevolent mood.

Phillip's addiction to alcohol was the least of his vices. The only child of a wealthy St. Augustine couple, he was coddled by an indulgent, overprotective mother then verbally abused and saddled with high expectations by a distant, demanding father. From his dysfunctional family he learned early to use his intelligence, good looks, position, money, and lies to manipulate anyone and all situations to his advantage. Similar to the sociopath, Phillip lacked a conscience or concern for anything apart from their role in satisfying his personal agenda.

Over the years, Phillip alienated those around him. Now, only strangers were taken in by his charming good looks and disarming demeanor. The nurturing instinct of many women left them easy prey until, inevitably, his serious drinking problem caused them to run. Abandoned by those he had abused once too often, only Eve remained.

Eve, a friend since childhood, had a brief, intimate relationship with Phillip many years ago, but that infatuation quickly turned into pity. His only friend, she now felt obligated to provide, within reason, comfort and care. She had, on many occasions, consoled a drunken Phillip, crying, talking of suicide, pleading for her affection. He frightened her but her nurturing instinct was strong; ever the optimist, she couldn't justify casting him away and, almost without thought, actually became proactive in efforts to awaken what little feelings of sensitivity to others he might have.

Always an animal lover, she had given Phillip a cat three years ago to keep him company and perhaps help fill the void in his lonely life. Phillip immediately became attached to the animal and cared for it lovingly. Ironically, he treated the animal with more love and consideration than he had ever extended to any person. But while the cat shared his life, it couldn't change the man.

Eve's relationship with Phillip was a serious dilemma for her because she knew Robert, whom she cared for deeply, detested Phillip and thought her stupid for continuing to support such a lost cause.

In truth, Robert feared for her safety because, though a spineless coward, he felt Phillip had the potential to do her harm, an idea Eve did not discount as possible, but still would not, or could not shake her involvement. It had caused many endurance tests in their relationship.

Phillip turned into his reserved parking place and entered the plush office. He punched the phone message machine and headed for the camouflaged liquor cabinet. He poured a double shot and started erasing messages as they finished, making mental notes to call or do something as each played and, in predictable fashion, would not follow through.

He stopped when he heard the voice of a private investigator he occasionally employed. The investigator, Buck, said he had the pictures he wanted, but he didn't think Phillip would like them.

"Shit!" He said out loud.

The pictures were needed to solidify a divorce case he was handling for an irate wife who was convinced her husband was keeping the company of a particular lady in town.

He poured another drink and reached for the rolodex, locating Buck's card, then dialed his home number.

"Hello," a sleepy Buck answered.

"Buck, Pena. What you got?"

"Damn, Mr. Pena, you know what time it is?" An agitated, but polite Buck responded.

"Well, you know what they say, Buck, no time like the present. What you got?" he repeated.

"Didn't have any luck with your guy. Watched him for six days. Nothing unusual. So then I decided to watch the lady he's supposed to be seeing and sure enough, she had a rendezvous at one of our seedier lodging establishments." Buck chuckled at his own humor.

"And," Phillip said impatiently.

"Oh, yeah. Anyway, she met a guy, and I thought at first it was your man; looked like 'em. So I took pictures. Then I realized it weren't him at all. Shore fooled me though."

"You sure?"

"I'm sure. I waited till he left and ran the tag. Ain't him." Buck paused. "Sorry. Might be he's a straight arrow," he added.

"How much like him does the other guy look?"

"Very close. But not him." Buck repeated.

"Send me the picture," Phillip instructed.

"What for? Ain't him."

"Buck, just send the picture, if you want to get paid," Phillip responded impatiently.

"OK. It's your money."

"That's right, and you should keep that little fact in mind if you would like to continue getting some of it."

"Of course, Mister Pena. I didn't mean to give you a hard time. Just wanna make sure you get the information you need." Buck replied defensively and with a gracious tone he definitely did not feel.

"OK, enough on that. What about the other job. You come up with anything?"

"The tail job, you mean?"

"Yes, Buck, the tail job. How many other jobs are you doing for me right now? What have you been able to find out?" Phillip replied sarcastically.

"Just a minute, let me grab my notebook so. . ."

"What notebook? I told you nothing in writing on that job; everything to me, verbally."

"Sure, Mister Pena, I remember. This is just little notes to myself. I use 'em to make sure I don't forget nothin'. I'll tear 'em up when I'm done."

"See that you do. Now, what do you have, particularly other people he may have visited and where and when they met."

"Sure, I remember. You want to know where he goes and who he sees. The short answer is almost nobody and nowhere." Buck chuckled at his own sense of humor.

"So you're telling me he doesn't go anywhere and he doesn't see anybody."

"That's 'bout it. He goes to work over at the college. Stopped by a store, different ones, a couple of times, and he goes home. The only place he seems to frequent kinda regularly is that little pub over 'cross from the fort."

"Louise's?" Phillip filled in the blank.

"Yeah, that's it. Louise's. Nice place. Been there a time or two myself. Anyway, he goes there a lot. Even walks sometimes."

"And he hasn't been to anyone's house or met anyone in town?" Phillip quizzed the investigator.

"Other than the stores and pub, only one other place; a house over on Sanford. Went there one day but didn't go in. Looked like he had a key, but he didn't open the door. I had to stay way back down the street, so I couldn't see too good, but it looked kinda like the key wouldn't work."

"Mister Pena?" Buck said, when Phillip did not respond.

"Yeah, Buck, I'm here. Just a minute."

After an extended silence, Phillip spoke again. "Ok, I want you to stay on him a few more days, and remember, no notes. Just report to me verbally. You understand?"

"Can do."

"One other thing, Buck. This person might have something that belongs to me, and I may want someone to get it back." Phillip waited.

"Ohhhh. I see. I know a guy could do that. Have to pay expenses though, he's out of town."

"That will be fine. Don't do anything, yet. I'll let you know."

Phillip hung up the phone and poured another drink. He thought about the divorce situation. Maybe the picture would be close enough to cast doubt and make negotiations easier. Worth a try, he figured.

Despite the alcohol's effect, Phillip's senses were reasonably clear. Clear enough to feel disappointment over Buck's report on the other situation; the 'tail job', as Buck had phrased it. Phillip knew he now must give serious thought to implementing the next step; or more correctly, have Buck and his friend implement.

Suddenly losing interest in paperwork he decided to go to Stewart's house and have another look around. He returned the half empty vodka bottle to the cabinet and left without turning out the lights.

CHAPTER 11

Robert snapped awake, looked at Eve sleeping peacefully beside him, and rubbed his face.

Glancing at the clock, he remembered his promise to start the inventory, so he decided to slip out and get to it.

He jotted a brief note to Eve and made his way quietly outside to his car. As he turned onto the street, he remembered Stewart's house key was on his desk. Well, I could do with a shower anyway, he thought, heading home.

By the time he arrived home, he had decided to shower and walk to Stewart's, by way of a breakfast café. He was famished! Wonder why, he smiled to himself. As he peeled his clothes off and checked phone messages, his eyes fell on the diary, still on the desk where he had left it. He picked it up and sat down, then turned to the last entry and re-read the brief note mentioning an argument. He flipped back toward the front and started thumbing through the pages.

March 12, 1892. Rec'd permission for
dig at old mission site. Crew
ready. Start tomorrow.

Robert flipped the pages slowly. Several entries about the dig and items being found. Then, April 4, 1892:

The priest representing the church
is very interested in dig. For this
reason, I receive good support.

Robert shut the book. Whoever made the entries wrote short and sweet. The time span of the entries made it impossible for the diary to have only one writer. Probably Stewart's father, maybe also an archaeologist, and then later, Stewart himself. That was the only logical explanation. Amazing, though, the similarity in the handwriting.

The ringing phone startled and reminded him he needed to hustle if breakfast was to be squeezed in. Deciding not to answer, he glanced at the caller I.D., then snatched the receiver from its cradle, dropping it on the desk with a bang.

"Eve," he said, regrouping.

"Well, that was interesting. Are you playing ball with the phone?"

He laughed. "No, I saw it was you and I became overwhelmed with thoughts of last night."

"Says he who crept out in the still of the morning."

"You were sleeping so peacefully, I didn't have the heart to wake you. . . great evening, Babe."

"Ditto. . . always is," she added.

"I'm thinking a kayak outing soon. You up for it?"

"Always. Call me."

"OK, Babe. Take care."

"You too. Bye."

Robert glanced at his watch as he hung up the phone. Damn! I need to get hopping, he thought, scrambling to the shower.

After a quick rinse, he dressed quickly, grabbed his canvas bag, and reached for the cigarette pack calling him from the desk.

"You lose." He said aloud, congratulating himself for winning the battle of wills. He turned toward the door, then remembered the diary. Thinking it might be useful during the inventory, and that he really should put it back, he shoved it into his bag.

As he rounded the corner to turn onto Aviles Street, a horse greeted him. The horse and carriage had stopped to pick up passengers walking in the street, a common habit for both locals and tourists in the Old Town. He diverted to the small sidewalk, nodding to the carriage driver busy helping his passengers board. Robert recognized him as the dark skin man from Louise's. Their eyes briefly met as Robert passed, recalling that he seemed to be seeing this guy everywhere lately. Not unusual though, since carriages did drive around all day.

"How long is the bridge project to last?" He asked as he entered Café Aviles where the dredge pounding one block over was still audible.

"Forever. Like all road work." Nancy answered without hesitation.

"Well, that's useful to know," he said.

"Another year and a half," she added flashing the famous grin. "You're lucky you don't live on the island. It's a pain some days." She glanced at a group of tourists banging their way through the door. "Order quick, writer man, if you want to eat."

"Oatmeal. I'm in a hurry."

"Coming up." She scurried away.

Thirty minutes later, he was crossing the street to Stewart's house, already focusing his attention on getting the inventory done.

"Back again, huh?"

Startled, he glanced toward the voice.

"Good morning, Margie," he greeted the old lady, busy clipping roses.

"This shore is a busy place lately," she said, continuing her search for the perfect flowers.

"Oh, how's that?"

"Another feller . . . 'bout your age—here early this morning. And last night that little, thin man was here. He couldn't get in though."

"What do you mean?"

"Key wouldn't work." She paused and straightened up. "He used to come and go all the time. They was friends you know. Other feller went in for a while, though."

Robert digested this information. Who was this friend? Probably couldn't get in because the locks had been changed. But apparently, the other guy did get in. Police, maybe?

"And what did you say this little man's name was?" He asked.

"Didn't say. Don't know. Not that friendly. Like ole' Stewart. Neither one very friendly. Seemed a little agitated though, when he couldn't get in."

"And how about the first fellow. You know him? Police maybe?"

"Don't know. Dressed nice. Suit and tie. Drove one of them fancy sports cars."

"Red?" He asked, immediately thinking of Phillip and his flashy Mercedes sportster.

"I believe it was." She squinted at Robert. "You know him?"

"Yes, he's a lawyer, Phillip Pena, handling the estate," he answered, wondering why Phillip had stopped by. Maybe to check on Robert.

Margie worked the clippers deftly.

"Well, gotta get to work. Nice seeing you again, Margie," he finally said.

"You too. Here. Might brighten things up in there," she replied, handing a rose over the small fence.

"Thank you, Margie." He sniffed the rose. "Have a great day." He turned to the door before she could respond.

Curious about the activity Margie had mentioned, he strolled through the house, trying to recall the placement of some of its contents. Seemed pretty much the same, he thought, entering the bedroom. He glanced around, turned to leave, then stopped. One of the drawers of the old chifferobe was slightly open. He opened it further, examining its contents. The old pocket watch and other items he had seen during his last visit were there. "Probably me," he mumbled, taking the items out to record and label, thinking this room shouldn't take very long, therefore a good place to start.

Several hours later, he stood and stretched, glancing about as he did so, pleased with his progress. Everything done except the artifacts. Deciding to consolidate those items in one place, he set about collecting them from various spots then placed them on the huge library table.

Leaning over and around an old, Spanish looking suit of armor to reach a shelf containing items, he nudged the large vest, sending it clattering to the floor with a bang. He picked up the rather heavy vest and breathed a sigh of relief when there did not appear to be any damage. He placed the uncomfortable looking object carefully on a chair, front side down to ensure it stayed there. As he turned it, he saw a small, cylindrical, cardboard tube taped to the underside of the vest. He removed it and walked to the desk where he opened the end cap and peered inside.

Rolled up pages. He fished the pages out, noting the very old, dry parchment type paper. Slowly, he unrolled the sheets to reveal faded words, scrawled in what appeared to be Spanish. Stuff for a museum, he thought, rolling the pages up and placing them back into the tube.

Leaving the container beside the diary, he reached for a cigarette and found instead his empty pocket. Crap! His immediate thought, remembering winning this morning's philosophical battle by leaving the pack on his desk.

Agitated, he picked up the diary and began flipping through the pages backward, having decided to take a break anyway before tackling the artifacts. He stopped at an entry made several days before the last entry:

N. thks someone following him.

Belvs someone knows.

I assured him that would be quite

impossible. paranoid!

So N and Stewart had secrets, Robert mused, wondering again if N was the little man Margie kept mentioning. Sensing his investigative reporter days coming back, he shut the book and turned again to the task at hand, suddenly anxious to label and list the remaining artifacts and be done with what had now become a chore.

Working nonstop, he finally labeled and recorded the last inventory item. He took one last look through the house, comfortable that everything was accounted for.

Feeling Louise's beckoning, he grabbed his old bag and gathered his papers. He placed the tube containing the old pages in his overstuffed bag, wondering how to handle it for the inventory. Call it old Spanish papers, maybe? A light flashed in his head. Opening his cell phone, he scrolled his phone list. Perez. He punched the numbers, congratulating himself on the obvious solution.

"Father Perez, may I help you?"

"Father Perez, Robert Robson. How are you?"

"Robert, how nice. I'm just fine. It's good to hear from you."

Robert had known Father Perez his entire life. The old priest had been his mentor and confidant for many years. He had, in fact, been the driving force behind Robert's decision to go into journalism. Over the years, they had spent endless hours debating the great works of literature, a process that evolved into sometimes deep philosophical discussions, and his steadying influence in trying times had been significant in turning the trials and tribulations of youth into meaningful purpose for Robert. He was for many the place to turn when life's bumps seemed overwhelming.

"I've thought of you often, Robert. I miss our little discussions. We should get together," the old man said soothingly.

"I agree, Father. It's been too long," Robert replied, apologetically. "Father," Robert said, feeling like a heel for calling out of the blue and asking a favor, "I was wondering if you could do a small favor for me?"

"Of course, Robert. What is it?"

"Well, I'm working on something and I have some old Spanish pages that I need to identify. Not many, and I was hoping you might look at them and tell me what they are."

"Of course, I'd be happy to. . . Are you working on a new book?" Father Perez added.

"Well, I am, but this is actually something else I'm doing. I just basically need enough information to name the papers. It wouldn't be necessary to translate all of it, just enough for reference."

"No problem. Send them to me, then maybe we can get together."

"That would be great. I'll be passing by your place in

a few minutes." Robert replied, thinking of his route to Louise's with a touch of guilt. "I'll stick 'em in your box, if that's OK."

"Fine. I'll call you after I've had a look."

"I really appreciate it, Father."

"Maybe I'll see you Sunday?" Father Perez asked, as more of a suggestion, than a question.

Robert smiled. He had not been to church in a while and he knew this was a gentle reminder from the old priest.

"I'm sorry I've been a little delinquent, Father. Sunday, it is!"

There was a chuckle on the other end. "Well, this worked well. Divine intervention, maybe?"

"You're probably right, Father, as always."

"I'll look forward to it, Robert."

"Thanks again, Father," Robert responded, making a mental note to attend mass Sunday, knowing how much it would mean to his friend.

Robert hung up, congratulating himself on the idea and took one last look around. He glanced at the diary, which he had planned to leave so Phillip could decide its disposition.

He stood, bag dangling from his shoulder, and contemplated the book. After a moment, he snatched up the diary, justifying that he could always bring it back.

He approached Father Perez's small rectory, and though he wanted to see his old friend, he felt a need for the somewhat different atmosphere of Louise's. He quickly dug the tube out of his bag and placed it in the old Cypress box which served as the priest's communication center, then scurried away to his destination.

As he passed the Bridge of Lions, it appeared the construction activity was done for the day. He noticed a lone figure adorned in hard hat and heavy work boots doing something along the row of large steel pilings. He diverted his course and stepped onto the heavy iron platform that snaked out parallel to the old bridge.

"Can't come out here, fella," the hard hat said as he saw Robert approaching.

"I'm sorry, I was just curious about these poles. How does all this work?"

The man glanced around, nervous that this dumb tourist was going to get him in trouble by being in the workplace.

"They're the support structures for the new span." The man removed his hard hat and scratched his head. "You really shouldn't be here though. Against the rules. Dangerous."

"You're right. Tell me though, how do you connect these things. Bolts or something?"

"Oh, no. These just hold the cement we'll pour, then they come out," the man replied, proud to display his knowledge.

"That must take a lot of cement," Robert said, encouraging him.

"Oh, yeah. They go down thirty feet into the floor. 'nough cement in one to build a Wal-Mart parking lot," he said, pleased with his analogy.

"Wow. That is a lot."

"Yeah, not the place to drop something you ever want to see again," the man chuckled.

"I think you're right about that," Robert answered, surveying the imposing poles.

Robert looked at the impressive piling, perhaps three feet around and very long.

He pointed to a piling surrounded by a narrow scaffolding system. An open chute type device protruded from its top. "Why is that one different?"

"Next to be filled. We climb up and stick the cement tube in and pump away."

"Ohhh, I see," Robert was impressed with the cavernous size of the chute mouth, perhaps four feet across. "Be hard to miss, I guess."

"Yeah, guess it would."

"Well, thank you very much. I admire your obvious expertise." Robert added.

"Well, don't know 'bout that. Just a lot of slow work," the man replied, pleased.

"Well, thanks again. Have a good day." Robert turned to leave.

Robert entered Louise's, already tasting the cold draft that would soon materialize from his favorite hostess.

A heated dart game caught his attention. Various comments from the patrons left no doubt the pressure was on the man taking aim. The dart was launched, followed immediately by hoots and catcalls as it missed its mark.

With a laugh, Robert turned toward the bar and saw Nathaniel. Depositing his bag and the diary on the counter, he took a seat beside the little man. "How you doing, Nathaniel?"

"Oh, Robert." He paused, glancing at Robert's pile on the bar. "Fine," he said, somewhat coolly.

"Boy, this is gonna taste good," Robert said, grabbing the offered mug from Louise. He took a long pull. "I enjoyed our evening. Hope I didn't keep you up too late." He finally said, breaking the silence.

Nathaniel sat silent for a moment.

"No, not at all." He nodded toward the book. "Are you working on something?"

"Not writing. Just another little job I'm doing," Robert said, glancing at the diary.

"Looks old."

"It is. Kind of interesting." Robert replied, attributing Nathaniel's obvious interest in the book to his history passion.

"Looks like a log or journal of some type."

"Well, sort of . . . Just an old book." He paused. "So how's the world of academia?" he added, shifting the subject.

"Usual. Trying to interest our youth on matters more important than surfing and video games."

"Now, there's a challenge."

They both sipped their drinks. Not speaking.

"Louise, could I please borrow one of your girl cigarettes?" Robert finally said, his resolve to not smoke today yielding to the uncomfortable situation.

"Well, I dunno. I wouldn't want to contribute to your lack of will power," Louise said jokingly, holding the pack in view.

"Everyone's a comedian," Robert said snatching the pack.

"Well, I must go." Nathaniel said curtly. He nodded to Louise, then Robert. "Goodnight."

Robert watched him walk out, moving in that funny looking walk through the crowd.

"Strange dude." Louise remarked. "You know him?"

"No. Really just met him recently."

"Yeah, saw you guys leave together the other night. Thought that was interesting too."

"How so?" Robert looked at her questionably.

"Well, he's been coming in forever. Never saw him talk

to anybody." She laughed. "Guess he was star struck, meeting a famous writer and all."

"Very funny." He took a sip. "What else do you know about him?" He added, knowing Louise knew something about everyone.

"Nothing. Gave up trying to talk to 'em. Just really keeps to himself." She looked reflective a moment. "Funny thing though. Several months ago old man Allen came in—you know, used to be the librarian at the college, eons ago, first one they had. Don't get out much—must be eighty. Anyway, he spots the little dude and calls him by name. Well, the dude says he's mistaken, don't know him. Anyway, he left and old man Allen says he was sure it was the Professor Fuller he knew at the college years ago, but figured he had to be mistaken because he looked just like he did back then." She watched for a reaction from Robert.

"And what do you say?"

"Well, old folks have time and memory problems, I guess. Shore seemed flabbergasted, though. I never caught the gentleman's name, so don't know."

Robert pondered this information. Mr. Allen obviously knew Nathaniel's name, and he did work at the college. Why would he be so secretive?

He lit the cigarette and took a deep pull, immediately feeling lightheaded. He held the slender, female designed burning stick out. "Makes me feel feminine. More sensitive."

Louise laughed. "Well, take more then, you're making my petticoat curl. "

An hour later Robert was making the slow trek home through the quiet streets, very tired from the long day, but somehow alert. It was a mood that made him creative. Shifting the diary from one hand to the other, he thought about the entries he had read, the dates. Who was Stewart? Who was N? He recalled Margie's description of the stranger, noting it could easily fit Nathaniel. An archaeologist and a history professor. That fit. And Eve said they knew each other at the school. Was there a connection? What was the 'secret' alluded to in the diary entry. Maybe some artifact? But those guys, archaeologist types, usually sought to share their finds. Obviously, Stewart and N argued. About a vessel or something, he recalled the diary entry. Sounded like one had it and the other wanted it. But what was 'it'?

CHAPTER 12

Circa 1600

The tall, tattooed Indian pushed his pirogue, a canoe-like boat, through the calm river with long, powerful strokes. His sweating, well-muscled body glistened in the sun. His loincloth lay in a heap on the floor of the pirogue; today, Cacique, the young Holata, chief of the Utina, preferred the freedom of his nakedness, enjoying the breeze caressing his body.

A large swirl in the water ahead caught his eye and he stopped rowing, at the same time reaching for the arrow stuck in the long, black hair that adorned his head. With a resounding thud as he released the string, the arrow sought the target, a large soft shell turtle. As the arrow struck its mark, he grabbed his tarroya, a large cast net, and heaved it in a large arc toward the struggling victim, watching it fall around the target. Quickly, he pulled the line and closed the net, hauling the now still turtle toward his pirogue.

His woman would be happy, he thought, as the full net hit his craft. The soft shell was her favorite from the bountiful river provider, as it had been his father's, the great chief, Antipola, dead some four years now, or presumed dead.

Cacique's father and a small party of warriors had simply disappeared while en route to St. Augustine at the request of Governor Corcoles. He frowned as he thought of the governor, a man he viewed as having no honor.

When his father had not returned for several weeks, his second in command, the tribal Iniha, after pressure from the governor struck a deal to allow a Spanish garrison and mission to be co-located with the village. Soon after, when it became clear his father would not return, Cacique took over as chief.

The governor, once regarded as a fair man, ruled the Utina and all tribes with an iron fist. As the missionary friars took the heathens into Christianity, baptizing them and assigning them Christian names, the governor curtailed more and more of their freedoms. By the time Cacique realized the mistake the Iniha had made in striking a deal with the devil, it was too late. Cacique knew an uprising by any one or two tribes could be repelled quickly by the well-armed soldiers. Any hope of banding together more tribes was very slim, given the individual group mindset of the Timucua tribes, a system that had worked well for centuries, before the invaders.

Nevertheless, the young chief thought often of the way it was and of his father, whom he had, and still, adored. And of the vessel. Cacique's father, the great chief Antipola, had been at his grandfather's side when he took the vessel from Cacique's battle fallen great-grandfather, promising it would not be used again, but would instead be protected and guarded by the Utina chiefs. The promise had been fulfilled until his father had disappeared with the vessel. Cacique did not know for certain whether or not the many stories about the evil caused by a drink from the vessel or the long life it gave were true. Still, he felt a sense of betrayal because he should be guardian like his father and grandfather before him, but the vessel was lost with his father, so all presumed.

Shaking his head to clear the unpleasant thoughts Cacique eased the pirogue onto the grassy shore to begin the short trip back to his village.

"Father, Father." Joseph, Cacique's young son was running toward him as he neared the camp.

"Yes, Joseph, look what I have," Cacique held the turtle high. "Why are you so excited?" he added.

"The friar is here," the boy stammered, out of breath.

"The friar lives here," Cacique responded.

"No, no, Father, not Friar Manual," he said, referring to the tribe mission friar, "your friend, Friar Pineda."

"Oh, Father Pineda." Cacique smiled as he pictured the chubby little friar he had befriended long ago. It was he who had baptized both Cacique and his son and had given them Christian names. Father Pineda was one of the few invaders he truly liked, and while Cacique had consented to the baptism, the new religion remained secondary to his tribal beliefs. There had been many discussions about this with the jovial, understanding friar.

"And how is our friend?" He asked Joseph, who also enjoyed the good friar.

"He is well, Father. He wishes to see our chief."

"Run back and tell the father he may share our turtle tonight."

The teenager turned and bolted down the trail.

He will soon be a man, Cacique thought, watching the athletic youth run. Cacique quickened his pace toward the village.

The rotund friar leaned back and rubbed his protruding belly.

"A wonderful meal. Delicious." He glanced at Cacique's woman. "The great Utina chief's wife has done well," he said, nodding his head to the dark-haired woman. Turning back to Cacique, he bowed slightly. "It would please me if Chief Cacique would walk with this humble man," the friar said with great formality.

Laughing, Cacique rose.

"So formal tonight, good friar, do I see a favor coming?"

"Never, my friend. But I wish to discuss a matter with you," the friar responded.

"Then, we will walk." The chief strode out of the hut.

"I consider the great chief of the Utina tribe my dear friend," the friar said as they left the village center.

Cacique, surprised by the friar's serious tone glanced down at the robed little man.

"I am pleased, for you are my friend as well," he finally said.

"There is a matter of great importance we must discuss."

Cacique did not respond.

"You are familiar with the magical vessel of the Utina chief," the friar spoke softly, his words stopping Cacique.

"What do you know of the vessel?"

"I have heard stories, as you have." The friar paused, then continued. "Do you believe the stories?"

Deciding he could trust his old friend, Cacique finally spoke. "My father and his father before him believed. There are many stories. They were honorable men."

"Yes, I thought very highly of your father, the great chief Antipola."

They walked in silence.

"Your father had the vessel when he left this earth?" The friar's words were more a statement than a question.

Stopping, Cacique turned to face the friar. "My father always had the vessel, and his father before him." He paused. "I should now have the vessel for we are the guardians." He glanced down. "The vessel is lost. That is good, for it is evil."

Cacique started walking again, but the friar held out a hand to stop him.

"It is not lost, Cacique. I know where it is."

Cacique stared at his friend in silence for several seconds. "Then you must tell me for I am the guardian."

"Yes, that is the purpose of my visit. Its evil continues and must be stopped. You agree?"

"It is I who should question your motives, Friar. I am the guardian. I know the promise." Cacique's face took on a very serious scowl. "Tell me where it is. This matter does not concern you. I must have the vessel back."

"Yes, my friend, you are right. It is your place." The friar shook his head. "But, it will not be easy."

"It does not matter. I have no choice," Cacique responded.

The friar took a deep breath, "Governor Carcoles has it."

"The tyrant in St. Augustine who tricked my people? How do you know this?"

"I saw him drinking from it in his office. It had the feather." He paused. "It changed him," he finally added.

"Then I must kill him and return the vessel to its rightful place," Cacique said without hesitation.

"No, no, my friend. To do so would risk his revenge and a great war. Many would die."

Cacique knew the friar was right.

"But how, then?" He asked.

"It must be taken silently, as a thief would do. I will help, but you cannot come. It must be someone you trust with your life and who would not be recognizable. Do you know such a man?"

The chief thought for a moment. He did not like this turn of events. It was his place to retrieve the vessel. But, he knew the friar was right. He was too well known. It would risk too much.

"I will send my son," he spoke softly.

"But Joseph is only a boy," the friar protested.

"He is strong and smart. Soon he enters manhood," Cacique said proudly. "I have spoken of the vessel many times with him. It is his place, if not mine."

Knowing it would be fruitless to argue, the friar relented.

"In five days, there will be a great ball in St. Augustine. The Governor will preside. He will leave the vessel in his quarters. In the early morning of that day, send Joseph to me. With nightfall, we will take the vessel." He paused and placed his hand on the chief's arm. "You must make sure Joseph speaks of this to no one. He is young," he added.

"He is the son of Cacique, Chief of the Utina. He will do it." Cacique spoke with conviction.

"Very well, five days, then. I must leave tomorrow."

The days passed quickly. Cacique had waited two days before he told Joseph the plan. His son was excited and eager to please his father, the chief. They had spent each day together hunting, fishing, and talking, with Cacique doing all within his power to prepare his son for the dangerous task. Now, the fifth day was here and Joseph was near the town of

St. Augustine.

As he made his way carefully through the early morning streets searching for the friar's small house, he tried to blend in, as his father had instructed. He carried a small bag of shells as a gift to the mission friar from his tribe just as Father Pineda had suggested to his father. His hunting knife hung loosely at his side. As he walked, his mind went over the cover story he was to tell in the event he was stopped by a garrison guard. Like many younger Timucua, he had a rudimentary grasp of Spanish, picked up from the priests and colonists.

Two soldiers were walking toward him, laughing and talking. As they came closer, one gave him a glance, noting the bag. Joseph's heart quickened, but the soldier, in response to a comment and chuckle by his friend, turned his attention back to the conversation.

Relieved, he spotted a small cypress and coquina house. The door bearing a cross that he had been instructed to look for verified the friar's house. Seeing movement through the small window, he glanced up and down the street. Satisfied no one was watching him, he moved quickly to the door, opened by the friar as he approached.

"Come in, my son." The friar glanced about nervously. "Your journey went well?" He added.

"Yes, Father."

"Good. Good." He searched for signs of panic in the boy's face. Seeing none, he continued. "Your father, the chief, told you of the plan?"

"Yes, Father, many times."

"You can do this task?"

"Yes, Father, I will return the vessel to my father, the chief."

"And do you have questions?"

"No, Father, I am ready."

The friar appraised the boy silently. His father was correct, he thought, noting the young lad's well-muscled arms and calm demeanor.

"Good," the friar finally spoke. "You must wait very quietly in the back room until nightfall. But first we will talk about the Governor's house and each room. I will show you the window. Look first in the room where the bed is. You will have only a few minutes. If you do not find the vessel, you must leave." The friar handed him a small loaf of bread. "If you are seen, you will say I sent you to get this bread from the bakery near the house."

Joseph took the loaf.

"Now go to the room. We have a long wait." The friar turned to the papers cluttering his small desk.

As darkness enveloped St. Augustine, the streets became deserted. Many of those not attending the governor's ball were in that area anyway to see the who's who and break their monotonous evening routines.

When he was certain the streets were clear, he blew out his candle and called for Joseph. "It is time, my son." He touched the boy's shoulder. "You are ready?"

"Yes, Father," Joseph responded with confidence.

"Good, then let us go."

As they neared the governor's house, the friar moved to the shadows of the small buildings lining the street.

Soon, he stopped and peered around the corner, looking for the lone guard he knew would be in the vicinity. He spotted the bored soldier and pulled back, turning to Joseph. "Now," he instructed the boy, "I will occupy the guard. When you hear me speak, move around the building, but stay in the shadows, and go to the back corner of the house. There, a window is open. After you have the vessel, move down the house in the shadows to the corner where I can see you. When you are sure the guard has his back to you, go back to my house. You understand?"

The friar touched the boys arm again and headed toward the guard. As he approached in the darkness, he intentionally dropped his small cross. "Oh, can you help me, my son," he spoke to the guard.

Recognizing the garrison chaplain, the guard hurried over. "What is it, Father?"

The friar caught Joseph out of the corner of his eye darting to the house.

The plan was working well. The friar kept nudging his cross with a foot while he and the guard searched for it.

Soon he saw Joseph working his way back down the house, apparently successful in his mission.

The friar grabbed the cross and stood to turn the guard's attention away, "Oh, I have found it," he exclaimed, speaking the signal for Joseph to make his run.

"You, there!" a voice yelled out.

Joseph squatted down.

The friar turned toward the voice. It was the garrison sergeant of the guard.

"Why are you away from your post, you son of a dog," he yelled at the frightened soldier.

"Sir, I, Oh, I . . ."

"My dear sir, I am so sorry," the friar interjected, "I asked this lad to help me search for my cross. It was all my fault."

"Forgive me, Friar, but this matter does not concern you." The sergeant turned to the guard. "This fool knows his duty. He was not to leave his post."

"But, surely, my son . ." the friar started to protest, but was again cut off by the angry sergeant.

"Please leave us, Senor friar. I must attend to this matter." He again turned to the guard, "You are relieved. Go to the barracks and send a replacement. I will stay on your post. You will be dealt with tomorrow."

The frightened guard hustled off as the sergeant moved to the governor's house, stopping a mere fifteen feet from the crouched Joseph.

The friar, moving slowly away as instructed, tried to think what to do when out of the corner of his eye he saw Joseph moving toward the guard in a semi-crouch, knife drawn.

Sensing the boy's movement, the sergeant turned, reaching for his flintlock. Joseph lunged and the two men fell to the ground, locked in struggle.

Though young, Joseph was bigger and stronger than the other man. As they grunted, thrashing about on the ground, Joseph slowly forced his knife toward the soldier's throat.

His eyes wide, arm weakening against the strength and determination of the heathen, the soldier cried out.

With a surge of strength, Joseph drove his weapon to the mark, holding it tightly as the soldier twitched, gasping in a last, futile effort to live. Then he lay still.

Hurrying to Joseph's side, the friar reached for the soldier's foot.

"Joseph, help me drag him around the building."

That deed done, the friar grabbed Joseph's arm. "Come, you must go quickly." The friar glanced at the bag in the boy's hand. "You have the vessel?" He asked.

"Yes."

"Leave it with me. The soldiers will be alerted and you may be stopped. I will bring the vessel to the village." The friar waited.

"My father told me to bring the vessel," Joseph finally responded.

"Joseph, be reasonable. You cannot have the vessel on you if you are stopped. I will bring it later."

Though very young, Joseph knew this made sense.

"Joseph, you must go. Give me the vessel. I am your friend."

Reluctantly, Joseph handed the bag to the friar, took one last look and hurried to the walls.

For several days the town was in turmoil as the governor frantically searched for the vessel.

He did not, of course, search the church. Even had he done so, he would not have found the vessel, buried in a small earthen compartment under the floor of the church by Friar Pineda.

As the days passed, the governor seemed to age at an alarming rate and soon fell ill. After two weeks, the friar was summoned to administer last rites to the dying Corcoles. Having done this, the friar retrieved his journal, never returned by the governor, and placed it in the bag he had brought for that purpose. Wrapped carefully in a box, he placed it with the vessel under the floor of the St. Augustine mission church. Now, his next chore and most difficult one— to convince Cacique that the vessel should remain in the friar's care.

The meeting with the Utina chief did not go well. While he was grateful for his friend's help and the safe return of his son, Cacique did not have the object of the effort—the vessel. He would not accept the friar's logic that the vessel was safer in holy hands where it could be kept from others. Finally, fearing for his life, Friar Pineda left the village and never returned. He was saddened that he had lost his friend, the great chief, and that men had died, but in his heart he knew the vessel and its evil must be kept from the hands of man. His loss, and his burden must be endured to that end.

Now, many years later, the old friar, racked with fever from malaria, was making what would be the last entry in his own journal.

> The fever in me is worse. I fear
> I have little time left in this world.
> I have served my country and my
> God with all my being. I have few
> regrets, but for the death of one
> man at my doing. It was not
> intended, and I ask forgiveness
> once again. I stole from a friend.
> For that I beg forgiveness. I pray
> my God will understand that these
> acts occurred to remove evil from
> this land. The vessel is hidden
> where I pray it will never be found.
> I go to my death with these
> burdens, but the evil that is the
> tinaja is now on holy ground,
> safe from man.
> For this, I pray forgiveness
> for my sins is granted.

CHAPTER 13

Robert moaned and fumbled for the ringing phone on his bedside table. He opened his eyes and scowled at the bright red numbers on his digital clock. Six-thirty! He had worked late into the night on the novel that was still trying to find purpose, and now his head was throbbing.

"Hello." He muttered, half asleep.

"Robert. Did I wake you?"

"Father Perez," he replied, recognizing his old friend's voice. "No, not at all," he lied.

"I looked at your pages. Can you come see me?"

"Already! I hope you didn't put off other matters for this."

"No, I was curious and couldn't sleep so I took a look."

Robert could picture Father Perez in the old comfortable study he loved so much, pouring over the pages.

"Well, that's great. You want to just stick 'em in your box, and I'll pick them up when I go out?"

"I didn't write the translation yet. Can you come by this morning?"

"Sure," Robert replied, surprised at the priest's sense of urgency. "What's a good time?"

"I'll be here all morning. Come as soon as you can."

"Sure. I can be there in an hour or so," he replied, thinking that he'd actually rather lounge around awhile but concerned over the priest's serious tone.

"I'll look for you," Father Perez replied just as Robert heard his call waiting signal beeping.

"OK, Father. I look forward to it." He pressed the call button.

"Hello."

"Robert. Kyle."

"Kyle, what's up?"

"You interested in a little work?"

"Always," Robert replied.

"We want to do a St. Johns River feature. One of those then and now things. Can we meet for lunch and talk about it?"

Robert thought about his promised meeting with Father Perez. Maybe he could take care of both in one outing.

"Can we do it early?" He asked.

"Sure. How 'bout elevenish?"

"Good, Café Aviles?"

"Great, See you there."

Robert cradled the phone and moved into his small kitchen. Noting with disappointment that he had failed to set up his coffee pot the night before, he pulled a half full carton of milk from the refrigerator, lingering at the door long enough to contemplate the disarray inside. Opting for the easy way out, he shut the door and poured the milk over a bowl of Rice Krispies. As he listened to the popping cereal, he sliced a banana over the energetic kernels, thinking again how time got used up so quickly. Half the day would now be shot, and he had hoped to continue writing. Oh well, he sighed, never enough time.

After the bohemian breakfast and a cold shower, he

grabbed his bag, threw the diary inside as an afterthought and headed out.

"Robert. Come in." Father Perez greeted him a few minutes later. "Let's go into the study."

He followed the old priest into the simple but warm room where they had enjoyed many discussions over the years.

Without fanfare, the priest motioned Robert to a chair and reached for the journal pages on his desk.

"Robert, where did you get these pages?" the priest asked, unfolding his small, steel rimmed glasses.

Robert explained the inventory and finding the pages, adding that he now needed to identify them for the estate sale.

"Does anyone else know about them?"

"Well, I don't think so. Stewart obviously had hidden them, for whatever reason, and I haven't mentioned them to Phillip yet."

"Maybe you could hold off on that for awhile." The priest said, catching Robert by surprise.

The priest reached for a thick book bound like a manuscript. He settled back into his chair and looked at Robert.

"This is a translated copy of a journal kept by one of the first priests to come into this area, a Father Pareja. Father Pareja is noted for his mission work with the Timucua, and he was also a linguist." He held up the yellowed pages. "I believe your pages are from this original journal."

Robert absorbed this revelation. "That's fascinating."

"Yes, Yes it is," the priest agreed.

"Now, Robert, first of all, I'd like you to consider letting me keep the pages."

Caught by surprise, Robert took a moment to comprehend the request.

"I'm sorry, Robert. You must think me mad. You bring me papers to review, and I ask to keep them." The priest said when Robert did not respond. "I assure you I have a reason for my request." He added.

"Well, I don't know, Father, they belong to the estate . . ."

"They belong to the church, Robert," the priest said, cutting him off. "Besides, you said Stewart apparently did not have family."

"Are you sure they're from the journal? Why would they have been torn out?"

"I'm going to get to that, but I want you to agree to keep our discussion confidential. I know I can trust you to do that."

Robert thought about the request, knowing if he said yes, he could never break his friend's trust. And, he was right; they were probably the rightful property of the church.

"Sure. If you think that's best, but why all the secrecy?" He finally responded.

The priest breathed a sigh of relief. He took a deep breath. "From this point on, our conversation is between you and me." He smiled. "Just like the old days," he added, recalling their many deep, philosophical discussions. "Agreed?"

"Yes. Agreed," Robert replied.

"Father Pareja wrote, among other things, several entries in your pages about a mythical drinking vessel held and passed on by the Timucua Utina tribe chiefs. They believed that the vessel extended one's life."

"A Fountain of Youth," Robert quipped.

Not amused, the priest continued. "Apparently though, the Indians came to believe that the vessel was also evil. It caused those who drank from it to change. Maybe the power. Who knows? But anyway, they were convinced no good came from it. Father Pareja wrote that a Chief Parucusi made it his tinaja—drinking vessel—and after that the Indians referred to it as hitiquiry."

"What does that mean?"

"Loosely translated, that is Timucua for demon or evil spirit."

Robert let Perez's statement sink in.

The priest cleared his throat. "Father Pareja also wrote that the Indians viewed it as hachitimo—their word for something supernatural; not of this world."

"What did it look like?" Robert asked, unable to think of a more intelligent question.

"There are, of course, no pictures, so I don't know. But it was engraved with a feather, the sign of an Utina chief."

"A feather?"

"Yes, a feather."

"What happened to it?"

"Well, sounds like several generations of Utina chiefs kept it in protective custody . . . didn't use it, but felt a need to keep it safe."

"Self appointed guardians, huh?" Robert quipped.

"Actually, yes. They considered themselves guardians of the vessel."

"So did any of those chiefs use it?"

"After chief Parucusi's saga and from Pareja's other writings, I'd say no. You have to remember Robert, this was the fifteen, sixteen hundreds. The Timucua had strong beliefs, and like most early Indians, they were somewhat superstitious. They would not want a demon from another world in them."

The priest removed his glasses and gave Robert a very serious look. "Stewart didn't have it?" he asked.

"No, at least I didn't see it."

Father Perez picked up another book from the table. "This is a copy of another journal which belonged to Father Pineda, a friar who took up Father Pareja's work some years later. It has been in the possession of the church since his death in the late 1700's. When Father Pineda was dying of malaria, he made his last entry. That entry was almost a confession in which he asked forgiveness for a man's death involving the vessel. He wrote that he had buried the vessel and Father Pareja's journal on holy ground where they would not be found. He apparently believed the vessel had some power and was evil."

Robert was dumbfounded. What a book this would make! He took in a long breath and exhaled loudly.

"So you're saying that my pages are from a priest's journal written in the 1600's, and it describes a story about a magic glass that extended life and was evil." Robert summed up.

"That's right."

"And Father Pineda's journal from the 1700's also writes about the vessel and he says he hid both it and Father Pareja's journal." Robert continued.

"Yes."

"You said the church had Pineda's journal all along. Is that right?"

"Yes."

"What about Pareja's journal, with the missing pages?"

"It was found during an archaeological dig at the original mission site in the late 1800's."

Robert could feel his writer's adrenalin rushing. This

was incredible.

"But what about the missing pages? How did Stewart get them?" He finally managed to ask.

"You said he was an archaeologist," the priest spoke quietly.

"Well, yes, but we're talking over a hundred years after the journal was found. He couldn't have taken them."

"I don't know. I'm just telling you what happened, as the facts suggest."

"But, Father, you seem to be suggesting that Stewart found the journal and tore the pages out."

Robert looked at his friend with a serious face. "You know that would be impossible."

Father Perez held up a hand. "No, I'm not saying that. I'm merely telling you what the journals revealed." He paused, then added, "And someone tore those pages out. Stewart had them in his house."

"Well, Stewart was an archaeologist. He probably came by the pages in his work somehow," Robert said.

"Why did he hide them? A man in his profession would share finds like that." The priest eyed Robert.

"I admit that is kind of strange, but . . ." his voice trailed off. He leaned forward. "Father Perez, you don't believe this thing had the power to extend life, do you? It's an old Indian myth," he added.

The priest sat in silence for a moment.

"Robert," he finally spoke, "you and I have had many discussions on things that are hard to understand. We simply don't have answers for everything."

"You do believe it!"

"I didn't say that. It is apparent that two priests from that era thought there was something to it," he said, gesturing toward the journals. "Something happened, events happened—hard to explain events, which they associated with this vessel." He paused again, then added, "I don't know."

The two men stared at each other in silence.

Father Perez stood and stared out his window. When he spoke, his tone was low, soft; as if speaking to himself.

"Power can be a source of evil. And men will do extraordinary things to protect power, or they may associate power with something that makes them possessive and sometimes ruthless. Those affected can conjure up explanations that may not reflect the facts, but do give one an idea of consequences. Sometimes, over the years, fact and fiction merge together. Maybe this is the case here. I don't know," the priest said again.

Robert contemplated his friend's statement, his entire behavior and found it worrisome.

"Well, Father, I deal in facts. This is an Indian myth. Stewart got the pages from wherever and decided not to share them. He sounded a little eccentric anyway." Robert said, thinking he might move the conversation back to reality.

"You inventoried the house so you saw everything there?" The priest questioned.

"Every nook and cranny," Robert replied, thinking of the diary.

"Did you see anything that might be this vessel object? Anything at all?"

"No, nothing. Lots of artifacts, but nothing remotely close to that."

The men sat quietly.

"Well, Father, this has been fascinating. Make a good novel," he added, laughing.

"Except we talked in confidence," the priest reminded him.

"Yes, of course. Just kidding."

"And, may I keep the pages?" the priest asked anxiously.

"Of course." Robert answered without hesitation, more than happy to do something for this old friend who had helped him so many times. "You're right. It is the property of the church and I think that would be the right thing to do. What will you do with them?" he added.

"I'm not sure, yet." He put his hand on Robert's shoulder. "Robert, should you find this vessel, would you tell me before you do anything?"

Robert pondered the question. He couldn't believe this very wise, scholarly man believed this myth, but he was definitely serious about the whole thing.

"Yes, I will, Father. I'll even have another close look around Stewart's house," he added.

"Good. Good." The priest seemed relieved. "Now, I know you have things to do, so I won't keep you any longer. Thank you for coming so promptly."

"It is I who should thank you, Father. I'll stay in touch."

"Mass Sunday," the priest said with a mischievous grin, as a gentle reminder of their deal.

"Yes, Father, Sunday," Robert laughed.

As he left the rectory, he decided to patronize the Café Aviles early for the morning coffee he had missed earlier. Might even clear his spinning head while he waited for Kyle to show for their lunch date. Indian myths, journals, magic vessels. All the stuff of wild imaginations—and great books, he thought again.

"Well, the deep thinker." Kyle's voice jolted Robert out of his daze an hour later as he sat pondering the recent revelations.

"Kyle, how are you?" He said, rising to extend his hand.

"Good. What are you reflective about?"

"This stupid inventory you tricked me into." He said to his grinning friend. "It's turning into a dark mystery, complete with mythical Indian stories, supernatural happenings and other such bullshit," Robert said dramatically.

"Sounds like a story." Kyle moved aside while the waitress set the menus on the table. "Matter of fact, you might tie artifacts in with the river feature we're here to talk about."

"Actually, I was thinking the same thing. Maybe a book." Robert was thoughtful for a moment."

"So, what do you need?" He returned to the present.

"Wanna do a kinda' what it was, what it is thing, and, of course, get in as much river history and mystique as you can. That's where old artifacts might tie in. Give Clifford a call and pick his brain. Maybe even a picture of old Clifford showing one of those old Indian things of his." Kyle said, referring to the many items Clifford had gotten from the river over the years.

"Good idea. Matter of fact, I better call the marina and leave word for him to call me." He reached for his cell phone and placed the call.

The two men spent several minutes discussing the article, then switched to planning a fishing trip they had discussed earlier.

"Shit, I gotta go!" Kyle exclaimed, looking at his watch.

Robert glanced at the wall clock. "Time flies when

you're having fun."

"Very original. See you later," Kyle said, dropping money on the table. "Business lunch," he added grinning.

"OK. Thanks. Take care."

A light rain, more a drizzle as they call it in the south, had started to fall though the early afternoon Florida sun still ruled the sky. Robert dug his small, collapsible umbrella out of his bag and headed east on King Street, bound for Stewart's house. His investigative juices were now flowing freely, having been opened with Father Perez's revelations. He thought about diverting back home to get his car as a contingency should a harder rain follow, but he felt an almost urgent need to look around the archaeologist's house again.

The drizzle had almost stopped when he arrived and stepped on the porch to shake the umbrella. He felt relieved when he glanced toward Margie's porch and didn't see the old lady.

Dropping his bag by the door, he surveyed the front room, then methodically, room by room, started looking for places a small object could be placed. He found several nooks and crannies, but no object resembling the vessel the priest had described.

After almost an hour, he stood again in the front room, arms crossed, thinking where else he might look but finally acknowledged he had looked everywhere. Foolish anyway, he thought. What if there were a vessel or whatever. It's just a stupid myth.

He remembered the diary. Snatching his bag, he went to the rolltop desk and sat down, digging out the book.

Before he could open the diary, there was a light peck at the front door. He leaned so he could see through the room door and saw Margie peering through the small round front door glass.

Stuffing the diary back into the bag, he grabbed the strap and headed to the door.

"Margie. How nice. I was just leaving," he said, using his quickly concocted excuse to avoid getting tied up with the old gal.

"Oh, I won't hold you up, I just brought you a piece of fresh carrot cake," she said offering a large hunk of cake, neatly wrapped on a decorative paper plate.

"Well, that's so thoughtful. Would you mind if I took it with me. I'm afraid I'm running late for an appointment," he lied.

"Not at all. You go right ahead." She turned to leave. "Better hurry, though, looks like the rain may get harder."

"I will, and thanks again, Margie."

True to Margie's prediction, the 'bottom fell out' as Robert approached his apartment. He made a mad dash to his covered doorway, congratulating himself on perfect timing. As he fumbled for his key, the phone started ringing. Thinking it might be Eve, he hurried in and picked up the receiver.

"Hello," he gasped, out of breath from his run.

"Robert?"

"Clifford. Yes, how are you?"

"Well, bettern' you, sounds like."

"Yeah, I was running from the rain," Robert laughed. "Are you returning my call from earlier today or is this coincidence?" Robert added, knowing it was sometimes days between the old man's trips to the marina for supplies.

"Yeah, got your message just now. Over here gassing up. Love to help you, come on out. Better be soon though. Looks like a front coming in a couple of days." Clifford paused. "How 'bout tomorrow? They say this little rain is just passing through, so might be clear before the real McCoy comes and it rains hard enough to strangle a frog."

Robert pondered this suggestion, remembering how full his plate had been the last couple of days.

"Tomorrow's good. I'll be at your place by eight." He finally said, deciding a break with his old friend was just what he needed.

"Sounds good. I'll have grits and catfish ready."

Robert smiled. Clifford ate grits and catfish at least once a day. "I'll bring fresh eggs," he said, knowing the old man's fondness for eggs, but seldom treating himself.

"Good. See you then."

Robert hung up the phone, already feeling more relaxed thinking about the prospect of seeing Clifford and getting on the river. He peeled off his wet clothes, toweled off and dug the diary out of his bag, unable to still his curiosity any longer.

Lying naked in a half sitting position on his bed, he began to flip through the diary again—this time with more focus. He needed to resolve his curiosity, to make sense of the day's torrent of fascinating developments. He turned the pages, carefully and slowly, again noting that it was really more of a log, with several days, or even weeks between some entries.

There were entries that were very brief and many used a personal abbreviation system which made them difficult to decipher. He stopped at one such entry:

Fd old jrnl and container at dig
site. Jrnl in old Spn. Container fst
unbkn obj fd.

After careful thought, Robert figured out this meant a journal and some type of jug or something was found and the jug was intact. He recalled his earlier conversation with Father Perez. Could it be?

He read further, relieved to see a more graphic entry about the item:

> Did not tell priest abt jrnl and
> Container which is probably a
> drink vessel of some kind.
> Know he will want jnrl right
> Away and I want to translte frst.

He flipped a few more pages with unremarkable entries, helper problems, rain hindering progress and so on.

Then:

> My young Minorcan asst. Pena
> told priest abt jrnl. He wants
> it but not thru trans, need help.

Pena. Probably one of Phillip's relatives, Robert mused. Then two entries later:

> Have enlisted a hist prof to hlp
> trans jrnl - exp in erly Fla and old
> Span. Stalling priest.

Robert turned the page:

> Jrnl fascinating. Father Pareja
> remkble man. Much info on Tim
> Ind. Interesting entries abt a
> drink vessel with some power.
> Blve it is my find because of the
> fther etching refer'd to. Prof
> very exctd.

Robert sat up. Stewart, or whoever before him, did find the vessel...and Pareja's journal. He turned the page, his heart pounding loudly:

Can't delay trning over jrnl any lngr.
Priest insistent. N & I fnshed transl.
We agreed to tear out pgs abt vessel.
Will deny and hope priest does
Not shut down dig.

After his last two days, Robert should have been exhausted, but he never felt more alive. Who the hell was N? And why did they tear the pages out? The pages referred to had to be those Robert found. His mind raced. Maybe they believed the story and wanted to keep the vessel, and its secret. And apparently the priest didn't know he found it—at least the diary doesn't say he knew.

Robert leaned back against his pillow, staring at the ceiling. These guys actually believed this myth—or so it seemed. Maybe even Father Perez, though he didn't say so. This entire thing is incredible, he thought. And what a hell of a story it would make. He grimaced and folded his arms across his chest, thinking about his promise to Father Perez to keep quiet.

He jumped when the phone rang.

"Hello!" He said impatiently, angered by the intrusion.

"Robert?"

"Oh, Eve. Sorry. I was deep in thought. What's up, Babe?"

"I'm deep in thought, too. About you. Why don't you come over and have a glass of wine?"

Thinking this might be just what the doctor ordered to relax him, he smiled, but then remembered Clifford and the river tomorrow.

"Sounds good, but I can't stay the night. Got to get up early," he said, quickly yielding to the thought of cuddling up with Eve.

"You always sneak out early," she laughed. "But I'll forgive you. I'm pouring the wine."

"I'm there," he said, jumping out of bed, the diary and its mystery slipping to the back of his mind.

CHAPTER 14

Robert shoved the throttle forward, and the powerful boat shot out of Six Mile Creek into the St. Johns River for the short trip to Clifford's. The wind was already blowing about 12 knots at seven thirty so fishing didn't look too promising. Probably just as well, Robert thought. More time to visit his old friend and pick his brain for the river article Kyle wanted.

Clifford made his home in one of the few remaining 'cracker' shacks. Located about a half mile into a feeder stream that merged into wetlands, the shack was accessible only by water.

Robert throttled the engine back as he approached the narrow stream leading into Clifford's place, careful to avoid protruding cypress knees. He looked up into the tall, dense cypress trees that lined the stream, and as always, he was struck by the majestic trees, a true miracle of nature. Slender, irregular trunks, small, almost delicate appearing limbs and evergreen type needles rather than leaves. Clifford had once explained that the small limbs were a key part of nature's design; built to splinter in storm winds so they could not provide swaying leverage that could crack the trunk further down or uproot the tree from its foundation of water and mud, a requirement for good cypress growth.

He cut the engine and drifted gently up to the old rickety dock.

A short, barefoot, wiry old man was coming down the walk, his old beat up baseball cap sitting crooked on his balding head. A faded pair of coveralls completed his attire, except for the torn, thin T-shirt that could be seen under the bib straps, displaying various size stains and holes.

"I smell fish frying," Robert said, handing a large grocery bag up to Clifford. "Brought eggs," he added.

"Good to see you, Bobby boy," Clifford replied, one of only two people who could get away with calling him by that name—the other, his father, had started that ritual at Robert's birth. He peered into the bag. "Looks like you brought more than eggs."

"Just a few little things." Knowing the rustic life Clifford lived out here, barely making enough money from crabbing and trotlines to buy necessities, Robert always brought a few extras on his visits.

"Well, that's mighty kind of you. Come on up. Let's get some grub."

As they entered the small structure, a weathered cypress shutter banged against the side.

The shack was a conglomeration of discarded boards, timbers, and pilings Clifford had 'rescued' from the river after each storm. It gave new meaning to 'work in progress'. No basic, planned design, its shape evolved as repairs with available materials were made. It defied every building code known to man and would never be allowed under strict, modern permit rules today, but that was largely ignored because of its location off the beaten path and probably due in part to officials who could see more than rules when it came to the true rivermen like Clifford.

"Not much good for fishing today." Clifford remarked matter-of-factly.

"Well, I'm sure you have some trap work that needs to be done. We can visit and talk about the article I told you about while we work on 'em."

Clifford chuckled. "Yeah, always got traps need fixin'. How's your dad?" Clifford added, inquiring about his lifelong friend.

"He's fine. Told him I was coming out. He wanted to join me, but had to take Mom up to Jacksonville for an appointment."

"Well, tell him to get his skinny ass out here soon. Been too long."

Robert laughed, knowing the great pleasure both the old men took in chiding each other.

While Clifford fussed over his small two-burner stove, Robert wandered around the shack picking up some of the treasures Clifford had retrieved from the river over many years. Robert had fondled most of them several times, but they still fascinated him. Some had been here in the same spot when he came to see Clifford as a boy with his dad.

"Cliff, I'm doing a job going through the stuff of a fellow that died and he has a lot of similar looking artifacts."

"Most of 'em Seminole or Timucua," Cliff said, glancing over his shoulder.

"Clifford." A shout came from the dock.

Clifford moved to the open door and peered down the dock. "Joseph, come in. Got breakfast going."

"Sounds good, Cliff. I busted a shear pin and paddled in hoping you might have an extra," the dark man replied.

"Still got that fifty Johnson?"

"Yeah, same one."

"I can fix you up. Have some breakfast first and meet my friend Robert." Clifford led the way back into the shack.

"Robert, meet Joseph Solano."

The two men eyed each other with recognition.

"I've seen you around town." Robert offered his hand.

"Likewise. I drive the buggies off and on when the crabs get slow," Joseph replied.

"Of course. That's it. Nice to see you again."

"You boys sit down. Grub 'bout ready," Clifford interjected. "Say, Robert, Joseph here is a Timucua descendant. You oughtta' get him in your story."

"Timucua! I didn't know there were any left."

"Greatly watered down," Joseph laughed, "but a few. Most have Spanish names—have for years."

He spooned a mouthful of grits. "You doing a story, huh?"

Robert sipped the strong coffee. "Just a little article for the Record about the river. Might be interesting to tie the Timucua into it."

"Well, I'm afraid I don't know much. Few old stories. Be happy to meet you in town one day to talk, though."

"That would be good. How can I reach you?"

"Just leave word and a number at the stables and I'll get back to you."

Robert couldn't decide if the man was serious or just being polite.

The three men dug into Clifford's breakfast, exchanging chit-chat. Robert thought about his discussion with Father Perez and decided to ask the Timucua descendant about some of the details.

"Joseph, did you ever hear an old Timucua story about some mythical drinking vessel that made men live longer?"

"Hey, Joseph, maybe it's that ole' shell I gave you a couple years ago," Clifford interrupted. He laughed, "Maybe

I should have made it my water glass, might of helped my old creaky bones."

Joseph, poised with a fingerling catfish at this mouth had frozen and was staring at Robert.

"Shell?" Robert asked.

"Yeah, old, worn conch shell. Joseph told me his folks used 'em to drink from. I didn't need another shell, so I gave it to him." Clifford said.

"Oh, yeah, that old thing. Took it to my dad. Made his day. Way back, a Timucua's cup or whatever he drank from was very personal. It was one of the few things that didn't get burned with them when they died." Joseph, regaining his composure, finally said.

"Did it have any design on it?" Robert asked.

Joseph chewed thoughtfully.

"Don't think so."

"Sure it did," Clifford interjected again. "Remember. Had a gator on it." He squinted at Joseph. "You asked me if I ever found anything with a feather on it. Never did though.

"A feather!" Robert stopped the spoon of grits halfway to his mouth.

"I did?" Joseph said, his brow furrowed in thought.

"Well, shore." Clifford bit off a hunk of fish and started chewing, looking at Joseph. "Damn, Joseph, I'm an old geezer, but I think your mind's going," the old man said innocently.

"Too much sun, probably. I do remember the shell though. Those things are very rare." Joseph began eating again.

Robert glanced at the two men, his mind racing as he recalled Father Perez's description of the vessel, sure he had mentioned a feather, sign of some chief—Utina, or something.

"Did you hear that story?" He looked at Joseph. "Maybe from your father?"

Joseph chewed quietly.

"No, I don't think so." He shifted nervously. "But there were lots of stories."

Robert studied the man, realizing he had obviously made him uncomfortable. "I'm sure there's nothing to it. Sure would make a great article, though." He finally said to ease the situation.

Recalling his promise to Father Perez, he took a sip of coffee. "Well, I'm not really sure where I heard it, or when," he lied. "I'm going through the effects of a guy who died, and he had several Indian artifacts. Made me think of it." He sipped again. "Probably something I heard as a kid." He felt bad lying so eloquently, but justified his words with the old 'doesn't matter anyway' theory.

"That the archaeologist?"

Surprised, Robert jerked his head up to look at Joseph.

"Why, yes. How'd you know that?"

"Saw the ad in the Record for the estate sale they're gonna be holding on Sanford in a few days," Joseph responded.

Good ole' Phillip, Robert thought. Hadn't even told me the date.

"You might want to come. Could be some Timucua stuff. I have no idea."

"Maybe." Joseph stood, rolling up his sleeves.

"Well, I better get that shear pin in before the wind gets nasty."

Robert didn't catch his comment because he was staring at Joseph's forearm and the well worn, stretched tattoo that was barely visible. He squinted across the table and was sure he could make out the shape of a feather.

"Need any help?" Clifford asked.

"No, no. Just take a few minutes." Joseph replied, leaving the room.

"Clifford, did you ever notice that tattoo on Joseph's arm?" Robert asked as the Indian's footsteps faded down the dock.

"The feather? Yeah, asked him 'bout it once. Said it was done when he was real young. Some kind of tribal thing." He looked at Robert. "Why?"

"No reason. Just curious." He paused. "You think he is Timucua?"

"You really are curious today." The old man studied Robert. "Probably got some in him. Looks Indian. Saw his father once, years ago, up here visiting. He looks Indian. Must be near a hundred years old now. Still living, though." He took a handful of breakfast plates to his makeshift sink. "Got that same tattoo."

"A feather?" Robert asked.

"Yeah, feather. Couldn't tell looking at it though. I asked him." He laughed, then added, "Guess I'm curious too."

Robert digested the information as he helped Clifford with the dishes. They worked quietly and soon had the chores done.

"Well, you want to try fishing?" Clifford asked.

"No. You're right about the weather, let's fix some traps and talk about the river. Need a couple of pictures too."

"Well, I'll have to change shirts for that," the old man joked.

"You're fine. We'll get the real Clifford," Robert laughed.

"Let's see how Joseph's doin'."

Joseph was lowering his motor foot as they approached.

"All done, Clifford, I owe you," he said.

"Naw. You know bettern' that!"

"I know. I really appreciate it though. Long way to the marina paddling," Joseph replied.

"Anytime, Joseph. Glad to help."

"Well, nice meeting you, Robert. Let me know if you want to talk," Joseph said, turning to Robert.

"I will. Hope to see you soon."

The two men watched Joseph make his way down the little stream, then headed to the traps.

"So what tribe?" Robert said as they gathered the ropes and floats.

"What?"

"What tribe is Joseph?"

"Timucua, told you."

"Yeah, but I mean what tribe of the Timucua?"

"Oh yeah. He did mention that one time." Clifford scratched at his beard. "Can't remember."

"Utina?" Robert asked, recalling Father Perez's story.

"Utina." Clifford's weathered brow furrowed as he thought.

"Believe that was it. Not sure though." He looked up from the trap. "Boy, you shore are curious 'bout all this Indian stuff."

"Well, Clifford," Robert said dramatically, "You never know where the next story might come from."

They both laughed and went to work.

"Well, that 'bout does that," Clifford said two hours later, after much conversation. He gazed at the stack of traps. "That should do me a while."

"Yeah, I guess I better get out of here before the afternoon rain." Robert responded, as he stretched his stiff back. "Let me get a couple of pictures. Maybe you fixing a trap, then a long shot down the dock."

"Sure, I'll comb my hair." Clifford laughed, rubbing his bald head.

"You wish." Robert opened his camera case.

"So, Clifford," he said, positioning him for the picture, "if you had that magic vessel, think you would use it and live forever?"

The old man pondered the question.

"Well, I dunno. Be tempting. 'Course I already lived a long time." He looked reflective. "Probably not, though. Man 'sposed to live as long as he lives. Naturally. Don't know what would be the reason to live moren' that." He looked at Robert. "How 'bout you?"

Robert thought for a moment. "Well, I guess it would be good to not be in a hurry—knowing I had plenty of time." He pictured himself writing book after book, unharried, with time at his disposal. "Guess I don't know, either. Anyway, we'll never know because if there ever was a vessel with such power, which of course is ridiculous, it's apparently long gone."

Clifford laughed. "That's for sure. But lot of strange stuff happens in this old world; hard to explain." He turned serious. "Shore am glad you came out, Bobby boy."

"Me too, Clifford. We need to do it more often."

"Well, I'm here. You come anytime."

"I will, Clifford. Promise."

Robert threw his gear into the boat and headed out into what was now a very choppy river. He couldn't get his thoughts off Joseph, Father Perez's story—all of it. He was

148

also thinking about the times he had seen the Indian over the past few days: in front of Stewart's, Louise's, on the streets. Coincidence? He shook his head. Man, must be getting paranoid—like N, in Stewart's diary, whoever he was.

CHAPTER 15

Joseph turned off the small asphalt road near Ocala onto a smaller, graded dirt road. He fought the wheel of his old truck as the washboard road handed out its punishment to the truck's exhausted shock absorbers.

He rounded a gentle curve and turned into a well rutted dirt driveway leading to a small frame house nestled under a large live oak at the drive's end.

A weary looking dog came from under the porch and barked feebly.

Joseph stepped from the truck as the dog approached with a low growl.

"Gator, you old fool, don't you know me?"

The half blind dog started wagging his tail when he recognized Joseph's voice. He knelt to scratch Gator's ears. "You still kickin', huh?"

"Still does his job too," a voice from the porch said.

"Hi, Pop. How old is this ole' boy now?"

"Must be 14 or 15. Maybe older. Can't remember." Joseph's father replied. "Good to see you, son. Thought you forgot where I lived," he added.

"Well, if you'd move to St. Augustine like I been trying to get you to, you'd see me all the time," Joseph responded, knowing the independent old man would never do that, though Joseph had tried to convince him many times.

"Too many people. I'm fine right here."

"Well, I worry about you out here, all alone, no phone."

"I got neighbors. Besides, what'd I do with Gator?"

"Gator can come."

"Well, we'll see. Come on up. Just made tea. Go in

150

and get us some."

"OK. Anything else?"

"No, just tea. Got some left over squirrel, if you're hungry."

"Where did you get squirrel?"

"Shot 'em yesterday. Where you think?"

"Be right back," Joseph said, shaking his head, wishing again his father would quit going off into the woods hunting, but he knew it would be a waste of energy to bring it up.

He returned with two glasses of tea and handed one to his father.

"How's the crabbing and buggy business?" the old man asked after a sip of tea.

"Crabs kinda slow. Been driving the carriages a lot. Got a few yesterday though." Joseph took a long drink. "Good tea. Saw Clifford. Remember him?"

"Yeah. The old man on the river, nice fellow."

Joseph smiled at his use of 'old man.' His father was ninety four years old, but still didn't see himself as old, though Joseph noted with each visit that he was growing more and more feeble.

"Yeah. He is. I broke a shear pin and he helped me out."

The old man scratched Gator's head, lying peacefully at his feet.

"I have the shell he gave you. From our people."

Joseph knew what was coming next.

"What of your search?" the old man asked.

Joseph studied his father. The old man's obsession with this stupid vessel thing unnerved him, but he always humored him.

"I always look when I'm in the old places, in St.

Augustine, and when there are exhibits. It is all I can do." Joseph answered, recalling the countless times they had had such discussions over the years. He never really believed all the stories, but his father obviously did and reminded Joseph of his responsibility to his people every chance he got.

"It is there, somewhere."

"Well, if it is, it's not in use and that's what is important, isn't it?" Joseph said gently, wishing he could make his father feel better in some way.

"We are guardians. We must always seek it, as my father and his father did. One day we will find it." He looked at Joseph. "When your son is ready, you must pass on this task."

Joseph thought about his encounter with Clifford's friend, Robert. The conversation had been in his mind since they met. It was why he came to see his father, to reveal there had been interesting developments, but now, he was hesitant to feed the old man's hope.

"Pop, I know this means a lot to you, getting the vessel back, but it has been so many years. There's no telling what became of it." He studied the old man's face. "I know it's important. The vessel belongs to the Timucua, but do you really believe in its magical power?"

There, he finally said it. He had wanted to ask that question many times over the years, but feared his father would be offended. His father was a very intelligent man. Always proud of his heritage, he took every opportunity to instill the same pride in Joseph, and other relatives, most of whom had long ago stopped regarding themselves as descendants of the noble tribe. But he was not eccentric. Joseph really felt that his father couldn't possibly believe the story, but did feel a deep sense of responsibility as a descendant of

Utina chiefs. This feeling seemed to grow more important as he grew older.

The old man still had not answered the question.

Joseph pondered his dilemma. He had discovered by accident, while doing work for an old lady in town, that there was a man who apparently had been around a long time. Joseph's brief inquiries had borne that out, and though he didn't really believe the story, he found it interesting that the man was an archaeologist and had few friends except for a history professor, who also, it turned out went back quite a few years. Now, the archaeologist was dead and Robert Robson, involved with his estate, had asked Joseph about the story. Joseph still didn't believe this extended life thing, but had to acknowledge the existence of the vessel was possible. There was starting to be too many coincidences. Should he tell his father all of this? Get his hopes up? That was the dilemma. Though he knew it was a pipedream, he would like nothing more than to produce this object that meant so much to this old man. But, he also did not want to set him up for a major disappointment.

"It is not important that we believe the story of our fathers. We are guardians of the vessel and we do not know where it rests." The old man finally spoke. He touched his son's arm gently. "You are a good son. You will do your best. That is all I can ask."

"I will, Pop." Joseph took in a deep breath and exhaled slowly, his decision not to reveal more made.

"So, Pop, why don't you come back with me for a few days. Do you good to get away." He laughed. "I'll take you for a carriage ride."

"Too many people. You stay here," his father answered, turning the table, as he often did. "We will hunt."

"I have a job, Pop. I don't think they'd like it."

A smile creased the old, weathered face. "Then I will hunt. You can catch the claws," he said, referring to Joseph's crab business.

"Deal. Then we'll trade deer for crabmeat." Joseph laughed. "Which reminds me," he added, "got more crab and fish on ice in the truck. I'll trade you for that helpless squirrel you shot." He slapped the old man's shoulder and stepped over Gator to retrieve the seafood, glad he had decided not to reveal all the coincidences that had been developing. What did the writer discover? Where did the strange little professor, Fuller, fit in?

CHAPTER 16

Nathaniel Fuller eased the old Buick into the tight, unpaved parking space, privately complaining about the adjacent cars crowding his allotted space. Always in a hurry, people today. They never seem to pay attention to their surroundings, and they certainly didn't consider others. Just moving too fast. So different from years past when it was all so much more simple. And his few acquaintances wondered why he just kept to himself, he scoffed.

He switched off the tired old engine and looked around the lot out of habit; without thought. Satisfied he was alone, he gathered up his large leather briefcase, soft and wrinkled from many years of use. A prominent brass border on the oversized flap glinted from the car's overhead light. Large brass, block letters—his initials—had once been within the border, but Nathaniel had removed them long ago.

He methodically locked, then checked his car doors and walked through the ornamental iron gate toward his cottage, a small plain coquina structure crowded on both sides by renovated monstrosities.

His street, though well off the beaten path, had increased in activity over the years, causing his cottage to somehow seem less charming, less secure. He had taken the cottage at a time when he needed less room and a change from neighbors who had become too intrusive. Now, it occurred to him more frequently that he would need to consider another move soon. People always became too curious.

Stepping onto his front stoop, he glanced around, then unlocked the door. Always a nervous type, he had become even more so the past few weeks. It was becoming bothersome.

He neatly dropped his out of season jacket around a heavy wood hanger and brushed imagined debris off the lapels. After surveying his wine rack, he selected a fresh bottle, opened it and placed it on a small side table. He purposefully looked from one window to the other, as if seeking assurance he was not being watched. Satisfied, he moved to the small, uniquely carved wood base that held an artifact. As always, he stood quietly a moment, contemplating the base and the contents of its secret compartment. His hand moved to the box, caressed its smooth, carved finish. He traced the curving design along the box's side until the box front sprang open. His hand was mysteriously guided into the box where he removed the vessel from its resting place. He poured the red liquid into the container, a feeling of relief already enveloping him.

Nathaniel settled into the sagging, overstuffed chair and reached for the thick, open book lying on the companion stand, then took a small sip. Eyes closed, he felt the warmth surging through his body, causing a slight tingling sensation. The ritual was complete.

A small tree branch fell outside the window, causing his head to jerk in that direction nervously. With a sigh, he took another sip, feeling more rejuvenated, but without purpose.

He set the container down and removed a small locket from his watch pocket. The worn, scratched front sprang open when he pressed the tiny latch. A middle-aged woman, hair pulled tight around her head in the fashion of that time, smiled up at him. A rare smile formed slightly on his face. He still missed Julia terribly, though many years had passed since her death. Her unnecessary death, he thought bitterly.

If only Stewart had not been so selfish. As Nathaniel had watched Julia age, he panicked, until finally, he informed Stewart that he wanted her to drink from the vessel. He vehemently refused, reminding Nathaniel of their long standing agreement. Too risky, he had stated with finality. Always a reserved, timid man, Nathaniel had pleaded for his understanding, but the selfish man was totally unreceptive, threatening Nathaniel with dire consequences.

When Julia had finally died, a remorseful Nathaniel left town, not caring whether he lived or died.

He had wondered around the state aimlessly, not sure where he was going or what he was doing. He was totally lost, and with the realization that other than Stewart, Julia had been the only person who shared his life, he became more depressed. He had no friends, no relatives. As the days passed, he could feel himself changing. He grew weaker, more frail and each time he looked in a mirror, a different person looked back; an older person. He didn't care at first, then as he grew more weak and confused, he felt panic. All those years in the grip of the vessel. As Julia had aged, he wanted to quit, to be normal, to grow old with his bride, but his resolve always weakened, as if he was not in control. Like now.

Within days, he returned and re-entered the unspoken share agreement with Stewart. Their already strained relationship now became one of cool toleration, out of necessity because of the obsession each shared with their unholy secret.

It was an uneasy alliance that continued many years, each living their own lives of seclusion, meeting only to collaborate on matters of history and to renew the sharing ritual that had become essential to that life.

Nathaniel had felt no remorse over Stewart's death, though he was partly responsible.

Their suspicion and distrust of each other had worsened with each passing day. They argued frequently, as they had done that night on an innocent walk across the bridge. The argument grew into a struggle and Stewart had fallen over the bridge rail. Nathaniel heard him yelling from the water but did not help him.

Now, ironically, he did feel a sense of loneliness. The men had spent so many years in their strange relationship, fearing other ties. A sick kind of dependency had evolved; forever controlling their wills, their lives, now strangely, Nathaniel realized he had no one.

The reclusive little man had become more paranoid then ever. He knew Stewart had kept the journal pages. And there was also that diary. Though he had never seen its contents, he felt that Stewart had probably revealed their secret on its pages. He should have searched for it right away, before those locks were changed. By the time he had worked up the nerve to go in the house covertly, both it and the pages were gone. He knew that either the writer or lawyer had them, but he didn't know what to do about it. And the man in the buggy. Was he following him, or was his imagination going wild? It was all too stressful for a man whose life had been so predictable and routine for so long. Ironically, he envied the fate that took destiny out of Stewart's control and freed him, but Nathaniel felt powerless to follow suit. He had only to give up the vessel, to fight the temptation of its power, but he was not a strong man. The lure was too consuming.

Nathaniel gripped the vessel in both hands, felt its compelling power as the peaceful warmth radiated through his ageless body. Usually partaking without thought, he more and more felt a sense of panic. Would it be so forever? To what end, if there was an end. He stared at his beloved Julia, as if seeking her counsel. But there was none. There was only him . . and the vessel, now his alone.

CHAPTER 17

The pink and white umbrella—pastel, no less—was absurd because of both its color and size. It was huge. A gift, half joke, half practical, from Eve after they had been drowned on his open veranda by a sudden afternoon thundershower. He did enjoy the sound produced when raindrops hit its taunt canvas top as they were doing now.

Robert yawned and stared out across Lake Santa Maria, watching the egrets foraging, oblivious to the rain.

He had spent a restless night tossing and turning, finally giving up an hour ago—five o'clock. The river outing yesterday had made him feel good, as it always did when he saw his old friend. But he just couldn't get this whole vessel story out of his head, and meeting Joseph fueled those thoughts. He re-read several diary entries, piecing together that information with Father Perez's story. A mythical vessel, extended life, scheming by men to possess it—to use or protect. Always with bad results. What had father Perez called it? The Indian word—hitiquiry—evil spirit. Sure seemed like it. And Stewart, the illusive N, whoever he was.

It was all so incredible and so unbelievable. The only thing missing was Ponce de Leon. Never did find that fountain of youth, old Ponce. Was the myth he pursued not water at all, but a drinking vessel? Probably never know that answer because old Ponce came well before the priest and his journal.

He stood and ducked inside to grab a cigarette. It was an automatic act, smoking. Like driving a car. Crank, shift, accelerate, and the car moves. A chain of events. Extract a cigarette, place it in your mouth, strike a match, inhale, and so on, until it lay squashed and smoldering in an ashtray. Logically, break the pattern—reach for gum instead—and the chain doesn't start.

He contemplated this logic, then lit the cigarette. He picked up the diary again, inhaling deeply, feeling the rush as his brain rebelled with a sensation of dizziness.

Ash fell on the old pages as he began aimlessly flipping. He blew the page clean, set the demon in the ashtray and continued turning the pages, stopping on a full page of text—cryptic writing about the dig. A splotch, like some liquid had been spilled and made the last few lines difficult to make out. Producing his reading glasses, he squinted at the half smeared words:

Nathaniel wants to know if
I have the vessel

Robert felt his heart pounding furiously and realized he wasn't breathing. He exhaled and squinted at the words again: Nathaniel. N was Nathaniel. He tore the page slightly in his haste to turn it.

and if I drk from it. Stupidly
I said yes. He demnded I
let him drk too

Robert turned the page back and looked at the date: May 2, 1892.

His head was spinning. His shaking hand retrieved the cigarette and placed it in his mouth. Coughing, he put it out and stood up, staring at the book.

Suddenly, he grabbed the diary and turned to the last entry, studying the handwriting, then back to the entry just read, then others.

The handwriting varied only slightly; sometimes appearing more deliberate. He looked at specific letters, searching for some uniqueness. Though not an expert, he was certain the same person made all the entries.

He sat down and calmed himself. This is bullshit! There's no way! I am caught up in the most incredible set of coincidences in history, he thought. This is the twenty-first century and I'm an educated, logical man. Maybe someone's idea of an elaborate hoax. No, that's stupid—too many actors.

He walked to the veranda window, watching the rain fall in sheets. There has to be an explan. . .

Riingggg.

Robert jumped at the sound of the phone ringing. Collecting his thoughts, he picked up the receiver, sending the instrument crashing to the floor.

"Hello."

"Damn, sounds like a party," Phillip said from the other end.

"Problem with the phone. What can I do for you?"

"You can tell me the inventory is done."

"It is."

"Good. I need you to bring your stuff and come over to Stewart's house. Someone broke in and we need to figure out what's missing."

"Broke in?"

"Yeah, apparently through a back window. Wasn't forced, so the police figure it was unlocked."

Robert digested this information.

"OK, I'll be right over."

Robert hung up and dressed quickly. He grabbed his bag then glanced at the diary but left it on the desk.

Margie was on her front porch when he arrived, curious about the police car and activity.

"What's goin' on, Robert?" she asked, as he ran for cover through the rain.

"Not sure, Margie. Just an old fashioned break in, I guess."

"Well, my goodness, who'd wannna' go in a dead man's place?"

"I don't know," he smiled in her direction. "I better go in."

"Mister Pena tells me you been doing an inventory of this place. That right?" A burly city policeman asked.

"Yes. Just finished a couple of days ago."

"Good. Good. You mind checking around and see if anything is missing?"

"Sure." Robert took the cataloging book from his bag and began moving around, though he recalled most items in the austere setting from memory.

All the artifacts were as he had left them. Even the old pocket watch and other modest jewelry he had moved to the table from the bedroom chifferobe.

He made his way from room to room, finally finishing in the bedroom. The chifferobe drawers were open, but other than that, everything looked the same.

"Nothing missing," he said, as he re-entered the living room where the cop and Phillip were talking.

"You sure?" The cop asked.

"Yes. I'm sure. Wasn't too much to start with."

"How about artifacts. Are you sure none of those are

missing?" Phillip interjected.

"No, they're all here."

"Well," the cop finally said, "not much to be done here. I'll file a report, otherwise, nothing else to do unless a neighbor saw something. Couple of my boys checking that now."

Robert thought about telling him about the little man Margie had seen on occasion. Maybe they could track him down. But he knew it was his own curiosity he was trying to satisfy. Besides, nothing stolen, so no need to bring Margie into it.

The cop turned to leave, "Oh, Mr. Robson, need you to drop by the station to do a report. No hurry. Couple days, OK?"

"Sure, I'll come later today."

"The detective investigating Stewart's death may want to talk to you later. He's out of town right now." The old cop eyeballed Robert.

"Oh, and bring your inventory so we can get a copy."

"No problem."

The cop left.

"Well, we'll go ahead with the sale. Cop said it was OK," Phillip said.

Robert looked at the lawyer. "Were you planning on telling me the date?"

"Oh yeah, day after tomorrow."

"I assume I need to be here?"

"Definitely. Plan on all day."

"Is that overtime?" Robert asked jokingly.

"Very funny. This is easy money, man."

He gave Robert a serious look.

"You're sure everything is here? You didn't take anything out to work at home or anything? I mean, if you did, that's fine. Matter of fact, if there's anything here you want, take it. No big deal." Phillip added, almost defensively.

Yeah, you son-of-a-bitch, I'll keep the diary, Robert thought, then said, "No, all present and accounted for. I might want to buy that desk chair, though. Would that be possible?"

"Take it."

"No, I'd rather pay for it," Robert responded, not wanting to be indebted to Phillip for anything.

"OK, how's seventy-five bucks?"

"That's fine. Can you deduct it from my fee for the inventory?"

"Can do. Get it out before the sale, though." He studied Robert for a moment."

"Cop said there is a secret compartment in that old chifferobe back there. You find anything in there, any artifacts or whatever?" He asked.

Robert thought of the diary.

"No." He lied, "Nothing but that pocket watch on the table."

They were silent for a moment.

"I mean it, Rob. If you took a little something, it's no problem. I just need to know in case something comes up."

Robert hated it when Phillip called him Rob. Too personal. Made them sound chummy, which they weren't.

"No, Phil," he responded sarcastically, "everything is here."

"OK. Good enough for me," Phillip said in a patronizing manner.

"Strange duck, old Stewart," he added, glancing around.

"How so?"

"Well, you know, eccentric," he gestured with his hand. "This old stuff. Just strange.

"You knew him?" Robert asked.

"Oh no. No." Phillip said, too quickly. "Just my impression."

"How about you, Phillip. I would think you'd want some of these artifacts, all that interest you had in Indians and such," Robert probed. "Unless you already picked out some," he added.

"What's that supposed to mean?" Phillip said defensively, agitated.

"Nothing. Just thought you being Minorcan and all, your family going way back, there might be some interest." He paused. "Any of your family ever involved in archaeology way back," Robert added, thinking of the diary and the writer's archaeology assistant, young Pena, and yielding to his fiction writer's juices.

"Archaeology!" Phillip said, surprised, "Well, you know, they did all kinds of things. . . but archaeology." He looked thoughtful. "Don't think so."

"Well, guess we can get out of here," Phillip said after an awkward silence.

"I'll load the chair and check around to make sure I'm ready for the big sale." Robert watched Phillip's reaction.

"You need help? I can look around with you."

"No, no. I have everything under control."

"OK, then. I'm gone," Phillip replied nervously.

Robert watched Phillip scurry through the rain to his red sportster and roar away, then went to the door as the rain started tapering off. Deciding to load the chair so he wouldn't have to return tomorrow, he propped the screen door open and rolled the chair onto the porch, then opened the rear of his old SUV and shifted the conglomeration of items around to make room. The chair went in with little hassle and he could already picture it setting where the bronco had reigned for years. Maybe I'll keep the bronco for guests I want to get rid of quickly, he mused.

He grabbed a towel from the bathroom to dry off and pictured Stewart shaving with the old straight razor. He suddenly realized he had no idea what Stewart looked like. Everyone had at least some pictures, but there were none in the house. He went to the old roll-top and casually started looking through the various items in the several little pigeonholes and miniature shelves that was the fashion in those days. Index cards, miscellaneous notes. A few old blank postcards, some stuck together. He had previously given them only a cursory glance. He started looking through the cards, carefully separating those stuck together. He paused as he separated one and discovered an old color depiction of the downtown area taken from across Matanzas Bay.

He dropped the card on top of the others but quickly picked it up again. Too heavy. Turning it over, he realized there was another smaller card stuck to its back. He dug his pocket knife out and carefully started separating the cards, grimacing as a piece stuck to the other card. He worked the knife blade slowly between the cards. They separated, revealing not a postcard, but a small picture. He studied the faded, brownish photo.

Three men, one standing in what appeared to be a priest smock and two others, kneeling. One wore an old safari type hat. Robert glanced at the coat rack in the foyer where the hat he recalled still hung. Same type. The man was average looking, big mustache, otherwise unremarkable. The other man, kneeling, was much younger. He looked familiar, but part of his head was blocked by a piece of the other card. Robert fumbled in the desk drawer for the magnifying glass he had seen. He held it over the picture and now realized why it looked familiar. The resemblance to Phillip was remarkable. Was this the assistant in the diary? Was the other man Stewart? He caught himself. Stewart's grandfather, maybe. The diary listed the assistant's name as Pena—same as Phillip.

Robert straightened up and dropped the picture. The entire scenario was getting ridiculous. This crap would make a Sherlock Holmes mystery pale in comparison. It defied the concept of coincidence.

Well, he thought, grabbing his bag, I've had enough of this for now. He started out, then went back to the desk and grabbed the picture, not able to resist the temptation to just walk out.

He left, determined to get through the sale and be done with the whole, strange mess.

CHAPTER 18

Robert crossed out a word he didn't like, replaced it, and forked the last piece of omelet into his mouth. He had been working on the river article Kyle wanted for the past two days and finally felt comfortable with his effort.

Looking at the wall clock in the Café Aviles, he moaned, acknowledging he really should get going. The estate sale at Stewart's would probably be an all day affair, so he had felt little urgency to arrive early. Besides, he justified, it was Phillip's show.

He slung the old canvas bag over his shoulder and started the fifteen minute walk to Sanford Street. As he crossed the parking lot behind the Lightner Museum, he saw Gene locking his patrol car.

"Hey, Gene. How you doing?"

"Rob. Good, and you?"

"Just fine, thanks."

"You taking your morning stroll?" The old cop asked, hooking his keys to a well adorned service belt.

"Yeah, kinda'. Got that estate sale today, over on Sanford."

"Oh yeah. Stewart. Shame about him, dying that way?"

"Yeah, it is. Any more on what happened?" Robert probed. "Do you still suspect foul play about how he died?"

he added.

The old cop scratched his jaw and raised his eyebrows. "Well now, don't know I really said anything about foul play. You hear that somewhere else?"

"Oh. No. I thought when we spoke before you felt it seemed suspicious. I just probably misunderstood." Robert backtracked. He grinned at Gene. "You're the expert, Gene. What do you think?" He added, hoping the schmoozing might bring out more information.

"Now, Rob, you know I can't say a lot about an active investigation. Besides, you might decide to write something 'bout it. Get us both in trouble." Gene finished with a big grin.

"No! You know I wouldn't do that, Gene."

"Yeah, I do. You always been an upfront feller." Gene glanced around, as if he needed assurance there was no one listening. He turned his attention back to Robert. "We don't really know much, 'cept it is a little suspicious," he added.

"How so? Why suspicious?"

"Just all so strange. Kinda' got the boys stumped."

"Why strange?" Robert persisted.

"Well, you know. Just couldn't find out much about him. Almost like he lived in a bubble or something. Just strange."

Robert thought of the picture.

"You said you saw him, didn't you, Gene?"

"Yeah, at the morgue. Kinda' messed up though. The water and all."

Robert pulled the old picture he had found at Stewart's from his pocket.

"This him, by any chance?" he said, showing it to the cop."

Gene studied the photograph. "May be some resemblance. Big mustache. Hard to tell, though, picture's so faded and Stewart's face kinda' messed up in the water. Kinda' hard to tell. Young feller looks familiar though." He added pointing to the assistant. He handed the picture back to Robert.

"Yeah, I thought so too," he said, taking the picture, again thinking about the strong resemblance to Phillip, and the same last name.

Gene took a red, bandana type handkerchief from his rear pocket and blew his nose. "The case detective talk to you about all this yet?"

"No, but I was told he might want to since I'm involved in the inventory."

"Yeah. Been out of town, but probably will. Just routine."

"Well, I guess I better get going. Good to see you, Gene." He said pocketing the picture.

"You too. Tell your dad hello."

"Will do." Robert responded as he turned to continue his walk.

When he finally arrived at Stewart's house, Phillip was explaining to a young woman how to log the sales and handle the money. There were already several people milling around.

"It's about time!" Phillip said when he saw Robert.

"How late do you need me?" Robert asked, ignoring Phillip's comment.

"Long as there are people here, in case something comes up."

"Fine." Robert responded, not very excited about that prospect. He deposited his bag in a corner and started casu-

171

ally moving among the people, some of whom he had seen around town, including the director of one of the museums. Probably came to check out the artifacts, he speculated.

He entered the back bedroom where three people were busy checking the austere furnishings. One was occupied checking out the small drawers of the old chifferobe. Robert realized it was Nathaniel.

"Nathaniel, good to see you."

The little man flinched slightly when he heard his name. He turned from the chest, gathering his composure. "Oh, Robert," he spoke nervously, "how are you?"

"Good, thank you." Robert said, strangely realizing he always felt the need to be very proper when speaking with Nathaniel.

"I'm not surprised to see you here. What do you think of the artifacts?"

The little man's eyes narrowed slightly at Robert's comment. "I saw the announcement in the Record and thought perhaps there might be something of interest." He paused, glancing around. "You too, I guess," he added.

"Well, no, not really. I inventoried the contents for a friend, so I have to be here." Robert embellished the truth.

"Oh, I see. And are the artifacts on the front room table all that were here?"

"Yes. That's pretty much it." Robert realized his intentional answer sounded inconclusive.

"Were there any historical papers, logs, that sort of thing? I know Stewart was an archaeologist."

Robert thought of the diary and journal pages.

"No. No. This is it." He finally responded, aware that Nathaniel was watching his reaction closely. "You knew Stewart, didn't you?" He added.

Nathaniel shifted uncomfortably. "Oh no, only occasional encounters at the college," he replied, too quickly.

Robert decided to raise the ante.

"Is this Stewart?" He asked, holding up the photograph he took from his pocket for Nathaniel to see.

The little man blushed. Small beads of sweat lined his brow.

"I . . . Stewart . . . I, oh, no, I don't think so." He mumbled, trying to regain his composure. "Some resemblance, perhaps, but, no I think not." He added, his voice returning to a normal level. "Was this in the house?"

Robert was silent for a moment, his eyes never leaving Nathaniel, a maneuver he had seen cops use during his reporter days.

"It was, yes." He finally spoke. "Look around as long as you like. Never know what you might find."

"Thank you, but I just stopped for a moment on my way to Gainesville for an overnight visit."

"Oh, my old college town. Do you go there often?"

"No, not often. I'm attending a seminar on Florida Indians. A visiting professor there has expertise on the significance of bird feathers to most American Indians. I thought it might be informative."

But Robert didn't catch the last part of Nathaniel's response. There were flashes in his brain; his head was spinning.

A feather!

That was the etching on the thing in the box at Nathaniel's. It was a feather, not a leaf as he had first thought. Why didn't he think of that before? And the object he had only seen briefly. . . Could it have been something to drink from? Yes! He silently answered his own question.

Nathaniel has the vessel; tinaja, a voice yelled in his head.

"Well, I must be off. Goodbye, Robert."

Robert realized Nathaniel had spoken, and was turning to leave.

"Oh, ah, yes," he stammered, still stunned by his own sudden revelation. "Have a safe trip." He finally managed to add. He watched the funny little walk as Nathaniel left the room.

Margie! Margie saw whoever came to see Stewart occasionally. Robert darted out the back door, hurried through the gate and ran up to Margie's back door where he knocked loudly.

He could hear the old woman talking as she moved at an incredibly slow pace to her rear door. Finally, it opened.

"Robert, what a surprise. I saw all the activity . . ."

"Margie, could we go to your front porch for a moment?" Robert tried to keep his voice civil as he cut her off.

Margie surveyed him with a questioning look. "Sure, come on through," she finally said.

Robert hurried the old woman through the house as quickly as possible, hoping Nathaniel had not made it to his car yet. He opened the screen door and stepped onto the porch, straining to spot Nathaniel among the several other people entering and exiting the vehicles lining the street.

"Well, my goodness, Robert. You seem in such a tizzy." Margie followed his gaze down the street. "You looking for somebody?"

Satisfied and disappointed that Nathaniel had left, and he would not be able to point him out to Margie, he turned to the old woman and smiled. "I know it sounds silly, Margie, but I was chatting with a friend of mine next door about the garden club—she's very active—and anyway, I mentioned your beautiful flowers." He paused, deciding where to go from that lame story. "She was very interested but was running late for an appointment, so she asked if I could get your phone number to her so she could call you." He checked for a reaction. "So I thought I'd run over and get you and try to catch her before she got to her car." He gestured hopelessly. "But apparently she left.".

"Oh, how nice. I'd love to talk to the garden club ladies. I'll just write down my number for you." She went back inside, with Robert on her heels, now anxious to leave.

Margie's phone number in hand, he headed to Stewart's the way he had come, thinking it was a good thing he did know a lady who was active in the Garden Club. He made a mental note to be sure to ask her to call Margie.

He stopped just inside the gate and lit a cigarette, trying to shift gears from Nathaniel back to the sale. Besides, he thought, even if Nathaniel was the N in the recent diary entries, he certainly was not the N the writer enlisted to help translate the journal over a hundred years ago.

Dropping the cigarette to the ground, he grabbed his cell phone and dialed Eve at work.

"Dr. Johnson's office, how may I help you," Eve's pleasant voice answered.

"Eve, does professor Fuller read Spanish?" Robert blurted out without fanfare.

"What? Robert?"

"I'm sorry, Babe. Just curious about whether the professor did any work in old Spanish."

"Well, yes, he does. I think he's regarded as somewhat of an expert in Spanish and other early Florida languages. Even some Indian, I think. Why do you ask?"

Robert was silent, thinking. How many men who walked like an egret visited Stewart, and also could read and write Spanish?

"Robert?"

"Oh, sorry. Got interrupted," he stammered, realizing he had not answered Eve.

"Robert, what is going on?" She paused and then spoke hesitantly. "I was going to call you, but I knew you'd be upset, so . . ."

"Upset? About what?" He cut her off.

"Phillip showed up last night. He was drinking . . ."

"What a surprise!" He interrupted sarcastically.

"Robert."

"I'm sorry, I'm sorry. So what happened?" He asked angrily.

"Well, he was pretty drunk—I finally had to drive him home. He was a little incoherent, but he said things about 'Robert knows' and 'that stupid little professor has it . . .' What is he talking about? What are you involved in?" There was worry in her voice.

"Nothing. You know Phillip. He's a drunk. Probably thinking about this estate sale or whatever. I'm sure it's nothing." He hoped his explanation sounded convincing.

"Eve?" He said, when she didn't respond.

"Robert, please be careful. He just seemed so agitated and bitter."

"Eve, come on. You know how he is. Probably doesn't even remember last night. Besides, I'm here with him now and he's fine. Other than being his normal asshole self." He couldn't resist adding.

"I wish you two wouldn't be that way. It's so childish."

"Yeah, you're probably right. Anyway, how 'bout that little outing. This weekend?" He asked, trying to alleviate her concern.

"Sure. Let's do it."

"OK. I'll call you later with details."

"OK. Talk to you then." She hung up.

More coincidences. What the hell did Phillip know? Did he know Stewart? Nathaniel? Did he see the diary? Surely not or he would have taken it. What then? He thought about the picture and what was apparently the assistant referred to in the diary. The resemblance. The name. Maybe he kept a diary. Damn! I'm really letting my imagination run wild now, he fussed with himself. He rubbed his face and re-entered the house, now packed with gawkers.

As Robert stepped into the living room, a man was holding the front door for two ladies coming in. He then left and walked down the steps. Robert hurried over to the door to get a better look. It was Joseph, the Indian.

Well, he had said he might come by. He thought about saying hello, with the possibility of setting up a meeting to talk about the Timucua and perhaps to learn more about Joseph. Instead, he turned and made his way to the table where the young woman was struggling to keep up with purchases and her log.

He waited while she helped someone then stepped closer. "Say . . ." he paused. "I'm sorry, I didn't catch your name earlier."

"Priscilla," she flashed a big smile.

"Priscilla. That's pretty. I was wondering, the dark man in the vest who just left, did he purchase anything?"

She thought a moment. "Oh yes, I remember. No, he didn't get anything, but he did ask if there were any other artifacts, or pieces that might have been used to drink from."

"What did you tell him?"

"Well, there are none here, and told him I didn't recall anything like that being sold, but you were the one to ask." She looked at Robert in a disapproving manner. "But I couldn't find you," she added.

"Oh, yeah. Sorry. I stepped out for a moment."

"Anyway, he looked around for a few minutes and left."

Robert digested this information. "Well, thanks, Priscilla. I'll be more diligent. You're doing a great job." He added, trying to smooth her feathers.

She flashed the big smile. "Oh, well, thank you. It's getting so hectic."

He spotted Phillip and headed toward him.

"Looks like it's going pretty good." He said, as he approached.

Phillip straightened up from his perusal of the old roll top items.

"Oh, yeah. OK."

"Did you know Stewart?" Robert asked, ignoring whatever better judgment he had left.

"Stewart! No. I told you." Phillip answered defensively.

"What about that little professor who was here a while ago. Fuller." He watched for a reaction, now feeling like an interrogator.

"Fuller. No. Don't know him." Phillip answered too quickly. "Why?" He added.

"Just curious. Strange duck." Robert said, noting that Phillip had used Fuller's name.

"Do you know him?" Phillip asked, now interested.

"Oh, no. No. Well, only slightly," Robert added.

No response.

"Mister Robson." Priscilla's voice rang out.

"Well, looks like I'm needed." Robert walked away to assist the girl.

It was well after six when Priscilla shut the door behind the last shoppers.

"Now the fun starts." Phillip said to Robert. "Need you to compile a list of what's left."

"Tonight?" Robert cringed at the thought.

"No, couple of days alright?"

"Good, I've had enough." Robert said relieved.

"Me too. I could use a drink." Priscilla said, looking at Robert.

Robert appraised the very attractive young woman, feeling flattered.

"Yeah, I know what you mean. Unfortunately, I have an engagement, so mine will have to wait." He responded, choosing discretion as the better part of valor—and not wanting to give the eavesdropping Phillip any fodder for him to pass along to Eve.

"Oh, too bad. Maybe another time," Priscilla said, disappointed.

"Yeah, that'd be great," Robert said politely.

Phillip had been listening in on the conversation with a smirk on his face. He glanced around the room and turned to Robert.

"Well, guess that's it. You need a lift?" He offered.

"Oh, no, thanks. I need the fresh air." Robert responded, surprised by the offer.

"OK. Two days on the report, then you'll get your check, minus the chair."

"Fine."

They locked up and went their separate ways with Robert heading down the street toward Louise's, contrary to what he told Priscilla. Hope to hell she isn't going there, he thought.

The scene in Louise's was calm. Unusual, but not unheard of. He had found in his many years as a patron of several pubs, that they usually took on the personality of their routine clients, so when that loyal bunch was not in attendance, the mood was somewhat different, perhaps even not as comfortable.

After one draft failed to clear his head of the diary and the questions posed, he left and started the walk home.

It was a quiet evening. Not even any carriages moving.

He thought of Joseph, realizing he was disappointed that neither he nor Nathaniel had been in Louise's. Now that it was obvious he could not put the whole vessel affair out of his mind, he had shifted to a mode of discovery, his old reporter juices flowing freely. The shroud of secrecy made him even more curious. He laughed aloud, thinking that he had his own shroud.

He thought about stopping by Father Perez's. It wouldn't be the first time he had shown up at his friend and mentor's house unannounced. Even Father Perez seemed so serious about the whole thing. Did he actually believe the stories, or was it a philosophical concern that men being what they were, evil acts would follow any quest for something with that alleged power.

His friend's behavior had frightened him. The priest had shown an attitude of. . . alarm. He was such an intelligent man; a man of deep faith, but still, while he didn't actually say so, it was as if he believed the story. Or perhaps, the better explanation, believed that evil could be caused by those who might believe it.

Maybe I should go by, he thought. Might do us both good to talk about it. I do feel somewhat philosophical tonight, he mused.

Instead, he found himself standing in front of Nathaniel's quiet, dark cottage.

If Nathaniel did have this thing—this vessel—surely he wouldn't keep it in his house. Unless, of course, he did use it, believed in its power. He had commented at the estate sale that he was going to Gainesville, so even if he had it, he wouldn't leave it overnight.

He thought again of the thing he had seen in the little box. He tried to concentrate on the design he had seen briefly, again deciding it could definitely be a feather. Or was he forcing his mind to visualize what he wanted to see?

He glanced up and down the dark street, noted the lights in the few surrounding houses, all with curtains drawn. He could tell through the shadows of Nathaniel's porch that a window had been left open, the curtains fluttering in the slight breeze.

Even though Nathaniel had said he would be gone overnight, he could change his mind and return early. Robert stepped into the shadow of a large tree as the thought of Nathaniel suddenly appearing occurred to him.

He knew that what he was thinking was foolish, or foolhardy. But he felt more alive as the adrenalin surged through his body. Was it there? Was it the illusive vessel? He could slip through the window, use his cigarette lighter to look, to know once and for all. But to what end? What if there was something that may or may not be this illusive vessel; so what. All he could really accomplish for his efforts is what he already knew; that there was something with a design on it in the box.

He glanced down the street again, the adrenalin shielding the shock he should feel because of his thoughts. This is stupid, he told himself. But his legs, as if moving of their own accord, stepped toward the porch.

CHAPTER 19

The last week in April was unusually beautiful along Florida's first coast. The predictable April showers were not as frequent or severe as the norm, and the pleasant 70's temperature was made even more so by the Mantanzas Bay breeze which seemed to be intentionally making the weather the essence of the tourist bureau's brochure promises. Retailers who depended on visitor traffic were ecstatic. The Old Town was postcard perfect.

Robert had finally finished the estate sale logs, made more of a task by Phillip's obnoxious attitude. He promised himself he would never enter such a venture again—particularly when hustling lawyers were involved.

He and Eve went on the promised outing, and it was nice, but not as enjoyable as usual. Robert knew that was his own fault. He couldn't seem to shake the entire Stewart mess. He was nervous, expectant; generally, just off his feed, as Clifford would say. He knew why. He had simply let himself be drawn into a situation that caused him to think and act differently. He had compromised his principles and it weighed heavily on his conscience. The dilemma was—how to change that, clear his mind, so he could return his thoughts to more productive endeavors. Like writing.

After several days absence, he was currently hugging a barstool at the pub. He had been reluctant to patronize his favorite haunt but finally decided that was a bit too extreme. It was a place he enjoyed far too much to let recent events dictate his lifestyle.

He was finishing his second draft when Nathaniel came in. Robert saw him enter and briefly shut his eyes, hoping when they opened, Nathaniel would not be there.

"Hello, Robert."

It didn't work. Robert took in a breath and exhaled slowly, turning to greet the little man.

"Hello, Natha . . ."

He froze when he faced Nathaniel. Never the picture of health, he now looked tired, almost weary. And older.

Robert regained his composure. "Nathaniel, haven't seen you for a while. How are you?" Robert felt foolish for even asking the question.

"I've been in a few times. Haven't seen you though. Busy, I guess."

"Yes I have been. You know how it goes."

"I do, yes." Nathaniel smiled. "You seem to keep busy," he added.

They chatted like strangers for several minutes. Robert grew more uncomfortable, Nathaniel more aloof.

Robert tried to lure Louise into their strained small talk, but the pub was particularly busy so that tactic did not offer much relief.

"I think I'll take a table. I'm tired." Nathaniel suddenly said, without an invitation or gesture for Robert to join him.

"Sure. See you later." Robert said relieved.

He turned back to his drink, his back to Nathaniel. He tried to engage Louise in conversation again to relieve the tension he felt, but he could feel Nathaniel's eyes boring into his back.

Finally, the situation became unbearable. Robert paid his tab and left without even a glance at Nathaniel.

His pace quickened as he headed down the bayfront, the urge to put as much distance between himself and the pub growing stronger with each step.

An hour later, feeling more refreshed after a warm shower, Robert was mixing a scotch and water when there was a light knock at the door. Surprised to have a visitor so late, he opened the door. It was Nathaniel.

"Nathaniel. You're out late. Come in." Robert said, not happy with this development.

Nathaniel seemed even more frail in the light. He sat down, uninvited.

"Can I fix you a drink?"

"No, no, nothing." Nathaniel looked at him with a distant stare in his eyes.

The men didn't speak. Robert sipped the scotch while Nathaniel continued to stare.

"What brings you by, Nathaniel?" Robert asked, unable to tolerate the tense situation any longer.

Nathaniel continued to stare, not speaking.

Finally, Robert stood and looked down at Nathaniel, thinking he might intimidate the little man into speech, or something.

"I know you have it." Nathaniel finally said, in a shaking voice, barely audible.

"Have what?" Robert countered. "What are you talking about?"

"The vessel. The vessel is gone."

He stared, waiting for a response, but Robert could not think what to say.

"I know you took it. You saw it that night, didn't you?"

Nathaniel said, rhetorically.

"Nathaniel, what are you suggesting? That I stole something from you?" Robert raised his voice, demanding an explanation.

The little man did not answer. Robert felt anger, at himself and Nathaniel. And sympathetic.

"Nathaniel, you look tired, I suggest you go home and rest." He finally said, wanting to be rid of the pathetic little man.

"I don't want it back. I just wanted to warn you." Nathaniel took a deep breath. "I did at first. I panicked. But I'm tired. I'm tired of watching friends grow old and die."

He collapsed back in the chair and made a futile attempt to laugh. "Actually, I haven't had any friends in a long time. It became too hard to explain why they grew old and I didn't." He sighed. "I have no one."

"What about Stewart?" Robert had to ask.

Nathaniel flashed a look of displeasure. "Stewart was just like me. We tolerated each other, sharing our little secret." He looked reflective. "He wouldn't share it with my Julia . . . He . . ." his voice trailed off. "But that was a long time ago." He finally finished.

"Did you kill Stewart?" Robert knew he was committed now.

"It was an accident. We argued." He laughed again. "We always argued. We were both obsessed. It just happened. He's lucky." He said with resignation.

He leaned forward and met Robert's eyes.

"Did you drink from it?"

"Nathaniel, I don't have whatever you are referring to. And I'm quite tired of this nonsense. I want you to leave."

Robert walked to the door and held it open.

186

With considerable effort, Nathaniel stood up.

"Don't drink from it, Robert. It will change you as it changed me. The Indians knew. They protected it from people like us."

He stepped onto the small landing.

"I will die now, Robert, but it is not your doing. I should have died long ago. I'm ready to end the madness."

He turned to go, then stopped. "Don't drink from it, Robert. You must destroy it. Others will try to take it." He said without turning back.

Robert shut the door and poured another drink with shaking hands. He tossed it down and poured another. He paused for several minutes, cursing himself for ever getting involved in this mess. He had to think.

"Well, that was interesting."

Robert jumped and spilled his drink. He turned toward the voice.

"Phillip! What are you . . ." He stopped in mid sentence when he saw the gun in Phillip's hand.

Phillip reached behind his back and locked the door. "You really should keep your door locked, Robert."

Robert couldn't take his eyes off the gun in Phillip's hand.

"Funny how things get turned around, isn't it? I followed Nathaniel, thinking he had the object of our desire, but from what I just heard, looks like ole' Bobby boy has it." He said, emphasizing the name he knew Robert never liked.

"Phillip, you're crazy. Is this a joke?" Bad choice of words, Robert thought. Phillip was crazy.

"I want the vessel. Get it."

"Or what. You gonna shoot me?" Robert said, not believing Phillip had the guts.

"Maybe not, if you cough it up. Most definitely if you don't." Phillip said coldly, his eyes glazed.

"Doesn't matter either way, because whatever this vessel thing is, I don't have it. If you overheard Nathaniel and me, you know I told him that."

"I read the diary, Robert."

"What diary?"

"Robert. Please."

"Why didn't you take it?" Robert asked, resigned to the fact that Phillip knew Robert must have removed it during his inventory.

"I left it so whoever had the vessel would come looking for it. Figured it was Fuller. Spent a lot of money having him and Stewart's house watched. I planned to go retrieve it after you took the job, but you beat me to it. Interesting book, don't you think?"

Phillip was too smart to believe any lie about the diary, so Robert appealed to his logic. "Yes, I took the diary. And I read it. It's a fairy tale, this vessel thing. It probably doesn't even exist, and if it did, it's an old Indian myth. Surely, you don't believe that story."

"Too many coincidences, Bobby boy. The vessel was even mentioned in some old family papers that belonged to a relative who was an assistant to the archaeologist who found the vessel—Stewart."

"Phillip, there's no way a smart guy like you believes for a minute that Stewart is the same man who started that diary in the 1800's."

"I know it's worth finding out." He grinned "I might even let you have a sip, if you haven't already. Just think, Bobby boy, immortality!"

Robert felt a lump rise in his throat when he realized

he was dealing with an already emotionally disturbed man, and now one who was obsessed with getting his hands on the vessel. Phillip was a lawyer. He needed to appeal to his real world logic.

"Phillip, if you shoot me, you'll never get away with it. Think about it."

"Already have. I'm a lawyer, remember." Phillip said, as if he had read Robert's thoughts. "Everyone knows we see the same girl. It's the old love triangle defense. I came to see you, you were drinking," he gestured toward the drink glass with his gun, and continued. "We argued over Eve, you pulled a gun, we wrestled, gun went off, and so on." He grinned again. "And by the way, the gun isn't registered." His face settled into a superior expression.

Now Robert felt fear. He had known fear before in similar situations—Vietnam. But at least there, he was dealing with a rational, though cunning enemy, and he had help.

"Phillip, you have to believe me, I don't have this vessel thing. If you put that gun down and leave, we'll forget the whole thing." He finally said, in one last effort to convince Phillip.

Phillip pulled the hammer of the revolver back with a resounding click.

"I'm through talking, Robert. Get it." He said with finality.

Robert knew he was serious. He needed to buy time and create a chance to go for the gun in Phillip's hand.

"It's not here."

"I'm warning you, Robert, don't play games."

"I'm telling the truth. It isn't here."

"Why don't we take a look?" Phillip waved the gun for effect. "You stay at least four feet in front of me. No sudden moves. Are you clear on that?"

"I'm clear."

They spent the next several minutes searching the house. Phillip, always out of reach, directed Robert as he opened and emptied drawers and took things out of closets, until the house resembled the aftermath of a hurricane.

Finally, an agitated Phillip waved the gun in Robert's face.

"OK, asshole. Where is it?"

Relieved no further search would be made here, Robert knew he needed to get Phillip out of the house.

"About five blocks from here. Downtown." He lied.

"Where?"

"Lora's place." Robert answered, naming the first place he could think of that might create an opportunity to catch Phillip off guard.

"Lora's! The shop?"

"Yes."

"You don't really expect me to believe that, do you?"

"It's true. I was doing a story there and I kicked up a loose board in the attic. I hid it there." It was the only thing Robert could think of. He held his breath.

"Get your car keys," Phillip instructed. "If it's not there, you're dead."

CHAPTER 20

Robert guided the car through the sleeping town. He stayed alert for an opportunity to grab the gun, but Phillip kept it pushed into his side, hammer cocked.

He turned down the small, one-way street searching for help in the few cars still in the public parking lot across from the alley leading to their destination. No possibilities. He slowed as they approached the left turn into the small, dirt alleyway. The heads of two horses appeared at the parking lot exit, but stopped, the driver apparently hearing Robert's car. He made the turn and stopped behind the three-story building.

"If the door is locked, I don't know how else to get in." Robert said, as they approached the large door.

"Well, then, you better hope it ain't locked."

Robert held his breath and grabbed the large handle of the sliding door, not sure whether or not he wanted it to open.

The door slid open with a groan. Guess Lora will be pissed off, he thought, recalling her complaints about the employees leaving the door unlocked for deliveries.

"Get in." Phillip instructed.

They stepped into the half dark storeroom, lit only by a night light.

"OK. Proceed very slowly." Phillip said grabbing

Robert's shirt in a bunch from the back and shoving the gun deeper into his lower torso.

Robert went through the stockroom, out into the main store and up the small stairs leading to the gallery. He crossed the gallery and opened the camouflaged door leading to the other storeroom on the second floor. There were no lights on, but the large unshaded windows let in enough light from the outside security bulbs to make out objects.

He started up the old stairs to the attic, stopping at the top to let his eyes adjust. The large room was lit only from the outside lights on St. George Street filtering through the large, front plate glass window.

"OK, where is it?" Phillip pushed the gun even deeper into his back.

"Phillip, let's stop this nonsense and forget this ever happened. We'll sleep on it and talk tomorrow." Robert said, deciding another try at logic was worth the gamble.

"You asshole! You were bluffing. It isn't here, is it?" Phillip was very agitated. He pushed the gun further into Robert's bruised back.

It was now or never. They were standing next to the old elevator shaft. He heard Phillip shift his feet. In a quick movement, Robert whirled, intending to knock Phillip's gun arm away and throw him to the floor. But as he whirled, the loose board shifted and his foot slipped into the space between the foot high rafters. He felt himself falling, then saw flashes of light when Phillip brought the gun down on his head like a club.

Robert fell in a heap, grabbing his head. He felt his conscious mind closing down as blood oozed from his head. He heard shuffling and grunting in the distance, then blackness.

"Robert."

"Robert."

Robert heard his name from far away. He opened his eyes, but couldn't see.

Slowly his sight cleared. Then he felt the pain. He groaned, reaching for his head as he tried to sit up.

"Lie still a minute. You must have taken quite a wallop. You've been out a while."

The voice again. Who was talking?

He blinked his eyes several times and tried to focus. The figure kneeling beside him spoke again. "Can you hear me?"

"Joseph?"

"Yes. Try to sit up now." Joseph held his hand behind Robert's back and helped him to a sitting position.

He moaned when the effort caused his pounding headache to hurt even more.

"Can you stand? We need to get out of here."

"Where . . ." Robert suddenly remembered.

"Phillip. Where's Phillip. He's got a gun," he stammered.

"Phillip is dead." Joseph spoke matter of factly.

"What? How?"

"I saw your car turn in and followed you. It looked suspicious. Anyway, I got up here just as Phillip hit you. We struggled and he went over. Down there." He nodded toward the elevator shaft.

"Are you sure he's dead?"

"He's dead. You were out, so I went down and checked."

Robert groaned again. "Help me up." He said to

Joseph.

He stood and peered over the elevator shaft rail and could make out a dark heap below.

"How do you feel?" Joseph asked.

"I think I'm OK. Just a little lightheaded."

He peered over the rail again. "We need to call the police," he added.

"I don't think that's a good idea," Joseph responded.

"Why not?"

"Well, think about it. What will you say? How will you explain this?"

"I'll tell the truth," he snickered, "for a change. Phillip forced me here at gunpoint and threatened to kill me. We struggled and he fell."

"And why did he force you here?" Joseph asked, obviously suspecting the answer.

Robert understood the point.

"You can't tell the whole story. The vessel seems to cause a lot of trouble." Joseph pointed out.

"So you do know the story." Robert said.

"Yes, I know the story."

"And I suppose you're a guardian of the mysterious vessel?" Robert asked, almost facetiously, recalling Father Perez's story.

"Yes, I am a descendant of the Utina chiefs—the guardians of the tinaja."

Robert stared at him for several seconds, suddenly very aware that Joseph presented yet another dilemma; namely, what were his intentions? He was a guardian. He would want the vessel. But would he kill for it? May as well see where I stand, he finally deduced.

"Well, at this point, I'd believe anything." He rubbed

his head again. "And do you believe the vessel myth?" He asked, taking the plunge.

Joseph met his stare.

"Well, I didn't. But I don't know anymore. I do know the vessel belongs to the Timucua—to my father. Do you have it? Is it here?"

Robert's second moment of truth tonight. He thought of Humphrey Bogart in 'The Maltese Falcon.' Like Bogey, Robert seemed to have something that everyone wanted; and some would kill for.

"If we don't call the police, what do you suggest we do?" He avoided Joseph's question.

Joseph stared at him in silence.

"Do you believe the story?" Joseph finally asked, catching Robert off guard.

"I admit there have been a lot of strange happenings and coincidences." He paused. "It's too incredible. I can't believe it."

"Can't or won't?"

Robert thought about this for a moment.

"Well," he finally said, "true or not, this vessel thing is dangerous to have around." He looked at Joseph. "And you're right. This would be hard to explain." He peered over the rail again. "We can't leave him here, though. That would raise too many questions. Cause Lora a lot of trouble too."

"I thought of that. I say we take him into the alley and leave 'em. Cops will think a derelict or unhappy client did him in. He was a lawyer, you know." Joseph added.

"What about the gun?" Robert asked.

"I have it. I'll throw it in the bay on my way back."

Well, that's great, Robert thought. Now he has the gun. He still could not determine Joseph's intentions, but once again, he seemed to have few alternatives.

"OK." Robert said reluctantly. "I need to get his keys so I can move his car off my street."

"Good idea."

It took several minutes to get Phillip's lifeless body positioned in the alley, but finally it was done. Robert felt like a common criminal, and he was wary that he might feel the gun in his ribs again at any moment, though his instinct was beginning to tell him that Joseph had his own dilemma, and he also struck him as an honorable man.

"I know this is bad," Joseph said, sensing his mood, and sharing the feeling, "but I can't think of any other solution."

"I know. You're right." Robert touched his head gingerly.

"Can you drive?" Joseph asked.

"Yeah. I'm OK."

"OK. I need to get these horses to the barn. I'm way overdue." His eyes met Robert's. "But we need to talk." He added in a serious tone.

"Yes. Tomorrow."

"You agree to do nothing until we talk?" Joseph said.

Robert studied the expressionless face of his co-conspirator. He knew they now shared a secret that made each dependent on the other.

"I agree." He finally said.

"I'll call you." Joseph turned and headed toward the impatient horses, pawing the ground to show their protest over the late feeding.

Robert listened as the last sounds of the horses' hooves on the brick streets faded into the distance.

He knew he should beat a hasty retreat from what was

now a crime scene, but he felt incredibly tired.

He crossed the alley and sat down on the old loading dock where he had stood with Lora just a few days ago. Much had changed in those few days. He almost smiled when he thought ironically that the last time he was here, in this very spot, his biggest problem was trying to get a stupid book review done. You truly don't know what tomorrow may bring, and he had certainly given new meaning to that old adage.

He needed to talk to someone. Father Perez. Eve. Kyle. Anyone he knew he could trust. But to what end? Complicate their lives too? No, it was his mess, and he had to resolve it, one way or the other.

With a slight moan, he struggled up from the rough dock timbers and headed toward his car and whatever another tomorrow might bring. At least, he remembered, he would have another tomorrow, thanks to Joseph.

CHAPTER 21

Robert woke with a pounding headache. By the time he had relocated Phillip's car and made the unsteady walk back to his apartment, he was exhausted and collapsed in his bed fully clothed.

He groaned, took a double dose of pain reliever and started a very strong pot of coffee.

He sipped the powerful coffee and was relieved when his groggy mind began to clear. His recollection of the events of last evening swirled in his head. What a mess! His face contorted into a look of disgust as he silently chastised himself for being such an idiot. While he felt terrible about Phillip, he took some comfort in the simple fact that Phillip caused his own demise, not Robert. And, Robert now had no doubt that Phillip would have killed him, an unbelievable shift from the somewhat cowardly Phillip he had known.

The ringing phone interrupted his thoughts. Damn, he thought. Probably Joseph wanting to meet and Robert still needed to sort out his mess. He moved stiffly to the phone and considered ignoring it but was spared that decision when he saw Kyle on the caller I.D.

"Hello."

"Robert."

"Kyle, how are you?" Robert responded, making a concerted effort to sound normal.

"Robert, Phillip is dead."

Robert's heart skipped a beat. Even though he was aware of Phillip's death, he still felt shock. Realizing that he also needed to express surprise and shock, he took in a breath and calmed his breathing.

"Dead! What happened?" He said, hoping he sounded surprised.

"Cops aren't sure, but definitely not by his own hand. They found him in that alley behind Lora's place. Neck broken."

"That's terrible." Robert said focusing all his concentration on sounding ignorant to the situation. "What do they think?" He asked the reporter.

"Well, his wallet with over two hundred bucks in it was on him, so not robbery."

Damn, Robert thought. He should have thought of that.

"Could be an angry client or adversary. Phillip was a little unscrupulous on occasion. Anyway, I knew you would want to know since you knew him well. Cops will probably want to talk to you."

"Yeah, I guess so. Damn. That's terrible." He added, trying to sound remorseful.

"I gotta run. Trying to put something together for tomorrow's paper—too late for today. Anyway, I knew you'd want to know. Sorry."

"Yeah, I appreciate it, Kyle. Thanks."

He hung up the phone, his thoughts already turning to Eve. He knew he had to call her before she found out some other way. He shook his head, knowing how upset she would be. He forced himself to dial her number.

"Hello."

"Eve, I have bad news." Robert licked his dry lips and tried to swallow.

"What's wrong?" she asked, the concern in her voice evident.

"Eve, I don't know how to say this. I was going to come over, but figured I'd miss you."

"Robert, what's wrong?" He could now hear panic in her tone. He took another deep breath.

"Eve, Phillip is dead."

"Eve?" He said after an extended silence.

"I . . . I'm here." He could hear her voice starting to crack.

"What happened?" She asked, her soft voice barely audible.

"He was apparently killed by someone. Kyle called me." He thought to add, explaining his knowledge of the situation.

He could hear her sobbing.

"Eve, I am so sorry. I know how you felt about him. I'm sorry I had to be . . ."

"Robert, you don't know how I felt." He could hear her struggling to fight back more tears.

"No, Eve. I didn't mean . . ."

"I just tried to help him." She cut him off again, anger in her voice. "You were always just so stupid and childish. You just never will understand." She finished, exasperated.

"Eve, you're right. I'm sorry." He said, feeling her pain, aggravated by his stupidity, which she had so correctly pointed out.

Her sobs were killing him, but he couldn't speak.

"I'm sorry, Robert. I'm not blaming you." She took a deep breath. "I knew his life would end horribly . . . It's just that . . ."

"Eve, I love you." He blurted out.

"I love you too, Robert. I hope you know that." She responded without hesitation.

His head was spinning. The revelation, spoken for the first time by both, seemed out of place. He felt happiness and remorse.

"Why don't you take the day off. I'll call you later," he said, feeling emotionally drained.

"No, I'd be better off at work. But do call me. Or come by later." She added.

"I will, Babe. You sure you're OK."

"Yes. I'll see you later." She hung up.

Robert went into the kitchen for another cup of coffee. He poured and stood sipping the dark liquid, tasteless for some reason. Scowling, he set the cup down, opened one of the top cabinets and removed a large round container of oatmeal. Prying off the lid, he stuck his hand into the flakes and pulled out the vessel, oblivious to the oats spilling on the counter and floor.

He set the object of his misery on the counter and stepped back, studying the thing; the cause of so much trouble and responsible for Robert's current dilemma. Where did it come from? Who made it? Why? It was unique looking, but there must be thousands of old, unique looking containers. There was something about this one though.

He moved back to the counter and touched the vessel, then rubbed its perfectly smooth finish, almost glass like to the touch. It looked so delicate but it obviously had survived for centuries—must be the magic part, he joked to himself. On impulse, Robert began to slowly tip the vessel forward until it fell to the floor, landing with a slight thud, intact. He picked it up and set it back on the counter, disappointed it did not break or bend. Now he ran his finger across the feather which he realized for the first time was not carved or etched at all. It was as smooth as the object itself. Couldn't be the crude paint Indians used for their bodies; that would have faded away long ago.

He picked it up again and looked into the smooth opening, then without thought, held it under the faucet and turned the water on. He watched the liquid fill the vessel. It was calming. He was mesmerized. Now full, water poured down the sides over Robert's hands. He felt a tingle in his fingers, then his hand, his arm. His eyes closed as he lifted the vessel.

Rrrringgg.

The vessel fell from his hand into the sink when he jumped, startled by the phone. He stared at the vessel, dumbfounded, then turned the water tap off.

"Hello." He said, expecting Joseph to answer.

"Robert, it's Father Perez. I just heard Phillip Pena was killed. Did you know?"

"Yes, Father. Kyle called earlier and told me."

"This is terrible. He was such a troubled man. What do you know about it? I know you were friends."

"Not really anything, Father. Just that he was found near St. George Street dead." Robert replied, deciding against correcting the priest on the friend part.

"Well, I'll go right over and see his family. You should too, Robert," he added.

"Yes, I will Father. Later." Robert paused. "Father Perez, I know this seems out of place right now, but I was wondering what you did with those journal pages." Robert hoped the old priest didn't think him unsympathetic, but he felt a need to talk with someone he trusted.

"I'm glad you brought that up, Robert. I was going to call you anyway." He coughed. "The pages are gone, Robert. I burned them."

"You burned them! But I thought you wanted them for church property, to complete Father Pareja's journal. Why on earth would you burn them?"

"You're right, Robert, that was my intention and I hope you don't think I purposefully deceived you, but I felt it was best not to share them."

Robert let this sink in. It was unlike his friend. He loved and protected anything historic, particularly church related. It was the vessel, Robert deducted. He didn't want anyone to read about the vessel.

"Father Perez, when we talked the other day, you never did tell me whether or not you believed any of that story. Do you?"

"It's not important, Robert. I believe there was, or still is, a vessel—the one referred to by the two priests and handed down for safekeeping by the Timucua chiefs. The priests and Indians saw it as evil. Men died because of it." He paused and took a breath. "Robert, what would you give to extend your life? To what ends would you go to obtain something that might help you do that? Even if you were not totally convinced of a promised power—of long life, if the opportunity was before you, would you take it? And if so, to what extreme would you go? Would you lie? Cheat? Kill? What would you do, Robert, if eternal life lay within your reach?"

"You're saying that even the possibility of extended life could be so tempting, the opportunity to have it should not even be given." Robert summed up.

"Yes."

"But, Father, there are so many temptations around. You can't hide everything."

"Robert, it's living forever. Immortality. That's different. You're a writer. How many books could you write in two lifetimes, three lifetimes? Would you like that opportunity?"

Robert considered the priest's words. To move at your own pace, never in a hurry because there would be so much time; that certainly would ease the suffering of writing.

"Well, I confess that would be nice."

"You see, you're tempted already, just as most men would be. No, Robert, the story may or may not be a myth, but to many, simply knowing the story and then seeing the chance to drink from this vessel, to possess that kind of power, would have no good end. The story is better left untold, unless you know beyond a doubt the vessel does not exist and it is only a mythical story."

Robert glanced toward his kitchen and pictured the vessel lying where he had dropped it. He recalled how strangely he felt as the water ran over his hands.

"I see your point. But it's a great story, Father."

"There are many stories, Robert. Leave this one alone. Give me your word."

"Father, that isn't quite fair."

"Well you think about it. Remember your history. Man's history. Leave the story alone, Robert." The old man cleared his throat. "Well, I must be off. Please let me know if you hear anything further from Kyle."

"I will, Father. Goodbye."

Robert hung up and returned to the kitchen. He dried the vessel and set it on the table. Maybe it is evil, he thought. I've lied, stolen and been involved in a murder since I learned of this thing—and I haven't even drunk from it! He thought about Stewart . . . Nathaniel. Unhappy, lonely. The tradeoffs for outliving those you love, the things you know. He thought of Eve. How would he feel watching her grow old while he lived on; but all that time to write, think—would it be worth it?

He snatched the vessel from the table and stuffed it into his canvas bag, as if that would make his dilemma go away. He recalled Nathaniel's words. On one hand, Robert felt responsible for the little man's state. He had obviously used the vessel; believed in its power. So much so, he now had resigned himself to dying. Was it possible that a person could believe something so deeply, it would change him? Even though logic dictated that the physical facts behind the belief were impossible? The philosophical question of the ages.

He could give the vessel back. Would Fuller take it? He had seemed almost relieved to be rid of it and resigned to his fate. Robert shook his head. Why do I have this thing! What now?

He thought again of Father Perez and wished he had sought his guidance, as he had so many times in the past. To what end, though? His friend obviously believed there was something evil about the object. Would he want it, as he had the journal pages? Would it tempt him? Hard to imagine, but it did seem to pull you in, weaken will. And what about Joseph?

They had not talked at length, but clearly, Joseph was interested in the vessel. He seemed skeptical about the truth of the story, but not the story itself. Would he try to take the vessel? To what length would he go? Joseph viewed the vessel as Timucua property and as a so called guardian descendant, seemed to take that responsibility seriously, whether or not he did believe in the vessel's power.

Robert forced himself to think logically, something he had failed to do lately, with this resulting mess. Joseph was the only person who knew Robert had the vessel, and he didn't know for certain, owing to Robert's evasiveness. He needed to resolve Joseph's position so he could sort this mess out. He glanced at his watch, surprised Joseph had not called. Impatient, he decided to go to Joseph.

CHAPTER 22

Robert parked between two of the stables' weather beaten barns. There was a flurry of activity. Horses being brushed and hitched to a variety of carriages, the more uncooperative being coerced by stable hands and drivers. Joseph was not among them. He spotted a ruddy faced, middle aged man with a clipboard, sure sign of a person in charge, and asked if Joseph had already left for his rounds.

"No. Joseph called in for the day off. Not like him to leave me short, but he said he had something important to do." The straw boss replied.

"Did he say where he'd be?" Robert asked.

The man looked at him questionably. "No, but he's a good man. Must've been important or he would be here." He announced curtly.

"Would you ask him to call Robert if you hear from him? He has the numbers."

"Sure," the man said, his attention diverted to a driver struggling to get a bridle over a horse that had other ideas. "Wait a minute," he yelled out, hurrying to the driver's aid without further comment.

Robert left and drove around aimlessly for several minutes hoping to spot Joseph. He now had a sense of urgency to get their encounter over with. When this did not prove productive, he thought about stopping for breakfast, but decided he really wasn't hungry. Finally, he headed back to his apartment to wait for Joseph to call.

Robert entered the house, his anxiety fueling the jumbled thoughts in his overtaxed head. Finally, unable to relax and tired of sorting through the myriad of dilemmas he had created, he turned to his primary outlet for shifting his mood.

Writing.

He turned the computer on and pulled up the new document screen. Without hesitation, he attacked the keyboard.

Several hours later, a knock at his door jerked him back to reality. He rubbed his aching hands, noting the page count on the screen—ninety two. Surprised, he realized how long he had been banging away, nonstop. He moved through the room to the door and saw Joseph through the window as he approached. Did I tell him where I lived? No, I'm sure I didn't, he thought. He opened the door, his anxiety returning in a surge.

"Joseph. I was wondering what happened to you. Come in."

"Had to go to Ocala." Joseph answered as he entered.

"Everything OK?" Robert asked, recalling that Joseph's father lived in Ocala.

"Yes, fine. Just needed to see my dad."

"Did you tell him what was going on?" Robert asked, not even considering that his question was forward and impolite.

"No. No. I didn't tell him. Just needed to talk." Joseph sighed. "He's very old."

"What do you think he would do?" Robert could not help himself.

Joseph forced a slight smile. "He would remind me of my responsibility."

"And what is that?" Robert asked.

"To get the tinaja. Return it to its rightful place."

"Then what?"

Joseph shook his head. "I don't know. I wish I did." He was obviously as perplexed as Robert. So many uncertainties.

Robert felt at ease with this man. He couldn't explain why. Maybe simply because he had saved his life. A sense of debt owed.

"Joseph, if the vessel exists, what would you or your father do with it?" Robert asked, wondering how much Joseph believed. He obviously loved his father very much. Would the old man use it? Would Joseph offer it to prolong his life? Stupid, Robert knew, but if you believed . . .

"I don't know." He said again. "I've given it a lot of thought. It's all my father thinks about."

"Maybe he believes the story." Robert paused, hoping he wouldn't go too far. "He's old, maybe he'd use it. Maybe you want it for him, to help him." Robert continued, searching Joseph's face for his reaction.

"No. No. He'd never use it. That's the point. He's a guardian." He shook his head. "As I am. Our responsibility is to keep it from being used. He would never use it." He finished, with finality.

"And you?" Robert asked.

"No. Whether true or not, I have heard the stories my entire life. Things you probably don't know. There is something . . . " He searched for a word. "Not real sure about it," he finished.

"What do you mean?"

Joseph's eyes met Robert's, unsure if he should continue.

"You know there is a feather on it?" He finally said.

"I've heard that." Robert answered, still feigning ignorance of the vessel's whereabouts.

"Do you know how it got there?"

"No, I assume carved or something."

209

"The vessel cannot be carved." He shook his head. "Or damaged in any way—so the story goes."

He swallowed and continued. "My ancestor, the Chief Parucusi, argued with the tribal toolmaker about etching the chief's sign on the vessel—a feather . . ."

"Like yours," Robert interrupted, gesturing toward Joseph's tattoo.

"Yes, like mine. And my father's, and his father before him. The mark of the Utina chiefs." He took a long breath.

"Anyway," he continued, "the toolmaker told him he couldn't do it, the vessel was a strange, hard material. Parucusi became angry and demanded he do it, the same size as the tattoo on his arm. He pressed the vessel over his tattoo to show the fit." Joseph stopped.

"Then what?" Robert prodded.

Joseph stood up and began pacing.

"When he removed the vessel from his arm, the feather was on it."

Robert stared.

Joseph returned to his seat and watched him.

"You don't believe that?" Robert finally managed to say.

"I don't know." Joseph replied, almost shouting. "I don't know. I've never seen it." He added in a quieter tone.

Robert recalled the vessel's smooth surface and the feather, equally smooth. Not carved. The object somehow had not felt as heavy as he thought it should be. At least based on appearance. Not metal, clay, wood, or any other material Robert was familiar with. Just different. Maybe that inspired the ridiculous story through the years; because it was so unlike anything the Indians had ever seen.

Typing the story into his computer while waiting for

Joseph to call caused him to conjure up an array of imaginative scenarios, including convincing himself to believe so the magic would work. He would never need to worry about time again. He liked the idea.

No one knew he had the vessel. Joseph surely suspected, but he couldn't be certain. He could just say nothing and the vessel would be his. Besides, if he used it, that would disprove the absurd story. He thought of Father Perez and the promise he had made. Maybe I should use it, then go to Father Perez, tell him it didn't work and make the old man feel better about the book Robert realized he had already started.

But what if . . .

No, he wouldn't even let himself think it. It was just too fantastic to believe, though he was forced to concede the vessel had a strange history—all bad.

He studied Joseph, sitting with his face cupped in both hands. Of all the players in this mess, Joseph has the biggest burden. His sense of loyalty to his father, his people. He had to know Robert had the vessel, still he had not pressed him, or held him at gunpoint, which spoke volumes about the man he was.

Suddenly realizing with crystal clarity what had to be done, Robert leaned over and touched the tortured man's arm.

Taking a deep breath, then exhaling slowly, he spoke. "Joseph, if you could tell your father that the vessel was in a place where it could never be found . . . could never again fall into the hands of man, would he accept that? Would you accept it?" Robert waited.

"The vessel cannot be destroyed. He wouldn't believe it." Joseph said, shaking his head.

"I didn't say destroyed. I said hidden." Robert repeated.

"It is always found. My father knows this. I believe he feels that is the destiny of the vessel."

"But you could convince him. My guess is he values your word. If you could tell him, without reservation, that it could never be found, would he accept that, coming from you?" Robert quickly added, "And, you could convince him that is better than being in the hands of any man, where it could be lost, stolen, or worse."

Joseph contemplated this scenario.

"You have it?" He suddenly asked, catching Robert off guard.

Robert's mind whirled. He had asked for the man's trust, now he was being asked to give his? All that he had said so far was 'what if.' Now, the question was before him. The answer would inevitably resolve his dilemma, but how do I want it resolved, he could not help thinking.

They both waited for an answer, eyes locked, hardly breathing.

"Yes. I have it." Robert finally said, feeling relieved about his proclamation.

Joseph stood again and began pacing. He moved to the window and stared out across the lake to the inlet.

"My people were the first." He spoke without turning. "This was their land. They hunted on the very spot where we are now talking. If the story is true, the vessel changed them. It caused many deaths in battle, it cast Timucua against Timucua."

He turned from the window, his decision made. "Yes, I will make him understand . . . accept. He will listen." He sat down again, searching Robert's eyes. "But the tinaja has been found before. Where is a place beyond man's search?"

"Before I tell you, do you want to see the vessel?" Robert asked, without concern, feeling the pact had been made.

"No!" Joseph said without hesitation.

Robert studied him with respect . . . and admiration.

"I understand." He said simply, and for the first time since he found Stewart's diary, he really did.

Epilogue

May 9, 2002

Robert took in a deep breath and exhaled.

The cursor on his computer screen continued blinking, awaiting his decision.

"Do you want to save this document?" It asked.

He was still not certain he believed or disbelieved the story. There were so many unexplained events. Men had died. Three in these past few days. Did he want to be responsible for more? He conceded that was possible in a world of deceit. And there was the detective who had questioned him after Phillip's death. Pretty shrewd, but Robert had managed to get through the interview without arousing his suspicion. But what if he read the story? And what about Father Perez and the promise Robert had made to him?

He moved the cursor to close screen. 'Do you want to save?' it asked. Yes or no? Damn, it's such a good story! Yes or no?

"Shit!" He yelled out loud as his hand directed the cursor to no and clicked.

"Well, that's that. Gone forever. I need a drink," he said to the computer. "Off to Louise's." He added over his shoulder as he left.

The fresh air felt good and he slowly regained his sense of humor as he walked, which eased the severity of what he had just done. He increased his pace as dark clouds started to form from the south.

The loud banging from the pilings still being pounded to the ocean floor for the new bridge reached his ears.

Coming right along, he noticed as he neared the activity. As he passed, he saw the worker who had explained the process to him a few days earlier. He was involved in animated conversation with two very official looking men.

Robert stopped as the worker threw his arm up and headed down the makeshift work float toward him. He could see the man was very upset.

"Hey, how you doing?" Robert asked, not sure if the red-faced man would even answer.

He glanced at Robert, not bothering to hide his current displeasure. But then, a glimmer of recognition.

"Oh, yeah. I remember now. The curious guy." He said.

"Yes. Good to see you. Looks like a little problem, huh?" Robert added.

"Not little!" The worker spat out, glancing back toward the two officials now joined by two more, pointing to the finished cement pilings jutting up out of the water.

"Those assholes makin' us take up two of those things."

Robert's mouth dropped open. His heart skipped.

"Gonna set us back days. Hell, probably weeks. Can you believe this shit?" He looked toward the pilings, shaking his head.

"'Course, all in a day's work or month's work in this case." He scratched his head. "Shore will set us back." He repeated.

"Why do you have to take them out?" Robert finally

215

asked, over the noise of his pounding heart.

"Said the sheets show the cement mix wasn't right for those loads. Tryin' to be oversafe, I guess."

"Well, how will you do it?"

"Cut 'em in sections as we pull 'em up. Lot of work." The worker wiped his forehead, as though the very thought tired him.

"Oh. So you'll cut them in pieces and let them drop to the bottom?" Robert, felt a sense of relief as he made the rhetorical statement.

"No, can't do that. Corps of Engineers won't let us." He spat out. "No, them monsters got to be sectioned, loaded, and hauled away." He appeared to be deep in thought, calculating. "We talkin' a lot of equipment; cranes, trucks, hydraulics." He shook his head yet again. "Lot of equipment."

"Where? What happens to them? Where do they go?" Robert blurted out, still unable to believe this unthinkable turn of events.

"Oh, hard to say. Some left together for pilings some-where else, some crushed into rock. You know, stuff like that."

"The crushed part. Where would that kind of rock be used?" Robert was feeling faint.

"Hard to say. All kinds of things: rock bed for a road, fill-in for mortar; might even wind up in your driveway. Hard to say." The worker repeated.

Robert looked at the monstrous pilings then back to the worker, remembering their earlier conversation.

Robert looked again at the pilings—ten up already— "Do you remember which one we were talking about that evening? Is it one of the two to come up?" He held his breath. Say no, please.

"Hell, I can't remember that! Can you?"

"No, guess not." Robert responded, suddenly feeling ill.

This was unreal.

He remembered Joseph's words. "It has always been found. My father says it is the destiny of the tinaja."

"Looks like rain. That's a fitting end to this day." The bridge worker said.

Robert turned, without answering and headed down the street. He soon found himself standing in front of Louise's.

Raising his right arm, he touched the small feather just above the underside of his wrist.

He turned and looked back toward the long row of pilings. A bolt of lightning flashed behind the old bridge as it started to rain.

Maybe Joseph's father was right? Maybe it was destiny . . .

He felt his body moving into the pub, away from the answer.

ABOUT THE AUTHOR

Randy Cribbs, a native of Florida, is a 2005 Much Ado About Books featured author. A retired Army officer, he holds degrees from the University of Florida, Pacific Lutheran University, Jacksonville State University, and is a graduate of the FBI National Academy and the Armed Forces Staff College. His works have appeared in several publications, and he is the author of four other books: 'Were You There?, Vietnam Notes'; 'Tales From the Oldest City'; 'One Summer In The Old Town'; and 'Illumination Rounds'. Shown above with Murphy, Randy resides in St. Augustine, Florida with his wife Sherry, where he teaches and writes.